PRAISE FOR *GOING ON BEING*

"Mark Epstein gets better and better with each book; *Going on Being* is his most brilliant yet. He weaves a mindful cartography of the human heart, tying together insights from Buddhism and psychoanalytic thought into an elegant, captivating tapestry. Epstein shares the spiritual and emotional insights garnered from his own life journey in a fascinating account of what it can mean to us all to go on being."
—Daniel Goleman, author of *Emotional Intelligence*

"Every element of Mark Epstein's brilliant and beautiful new book is on the highest level—the spiritual insights, the psychotherapeutic perspective, and his own very human story of wanting to bring greater awareness and love into his life. *Going on Being* opens a door on what it means to understand ourselves, to grow and change."
—Sharon Salzberg, author of *Lovingkindness* and *A Heart as Wide as the World*

"Mark Epstein's *Going on Being* joins the heart of psychotherapy with the heart of Buddhism. It takes us to freeing places, uplifts our lives. Honest, personal, searching—it affirms the goodness of our existence and encourages an openness that keeps us fresh."
—Michael Eigen, author of *The Psychoanalytic Mystic*

"A calm comes over me when I read Mark Epstein's work. His integration of Buddhist wisdom and meditative practice with the concerns and struggles of contemporary Western life reflects a seemingly impossible combination of rich, intricate texture with simplicity and vividness. *Going on Being* extends Epstein's vision and provides a personal memoir of his introduction to Buddhist thought in the context of transformative relationships with some remarkable men. There is a freshness and relevance to Epstein's vision

that makes this book a treasure and an important opportunity for anyone who takes their existence seriously (but not too seriously)."
—Stephen A. Mitchell, founding editor of *Psychoanalytic Dialogues: A Journal of Relational Perspectives*

"Through a graceful and generous recounting of his own quest for healing, Mark Epstein brings together certain core insights of Buddhism and psychotherapy in a way that is newly illuminating. The result is what Buddhists call 'a field of benefaction.' I felt happy reading this book. It will go—next to his two previous offerings—among the handful of books that I keep near me for those times, in the middle of the night, when I reach for true solace."
—Noelle Oxenhandler, author of *The Eros of Parenthood*

GOING ON BEING

GOING ON BEING

LIFE AT THE CROSSROADS OF
BUDDHISM AND PSYCHOTHERAPY

MARK EPSTEIN, M.D.

Wisdom Publications • Boston

Wisdom Publications
199 Elm Street
Somerville MA 02144 USA
www.wisdompubs.org

Library of Congress Cataloging-in-Publication Data
Epstein, Mark, 1953–
 Going on being : life at the crossroads of Buddhism and therapy / Mark Epstein.
   p. cm.
 Previously published: New York : Broadway Books, c2001.
 Includes bibliographical references and index.
 ISBN 0-86171-569-1 (pbk. : alk. paper)
 1. Buddhism—Psychology. 2. Psychotherapy—Religious aspects—Buddhism. 3. Aware-
ness. 4. Spiritual life—Psychology. 5. Epstein, Mark, 1953- I. Title.
 BQ4570.P76E664 2009
 294.3'42—dc22
                              2008041530

"Mind" from *The Dhammapada*. Copyright, P. Lal, Writers Workshop, 162/92 Lake Gardens,
Calcutta 700045 India.

ISBN 0-86171-569-1
12 11 10 09 08
5 4 3 2 1

Cover design by Pema Studios. Interior design by Dede Cummings. Set in Weiss 11/15.
Cover image © Vitalijus Majauskis.

Printed in the United States of America.

This book was produced with environmental mindfulness. We have elected to print
this title on 30% PCW recycled paper. As a result, we have saved the following
resources: 12 trees, 8 million BTUs of energy, 1,045 lbs. of greenhouse gases, 4,337 gal-
lons of water, and 557 lbs. of solid waste. For more information, please visit our website,
www.wisdompubs.org. This paper is also FSC certified. For more information, please visit
www.fscus.org.

FOR ARLENE

The alternative to being is reacting,
and reacting interrupts being and annihilates.

—D.W. Winnicott

CONTENTS

There is an obscure story about one of Freud's personal conversations that puts an interesting twist on the state of psychology in the West. The discussion was with Ludwig Binswanger, a Swiss psychiatrist and the founder of the existential movement in psychoanalysis. Binswanger felt that there was something missing in Freud's approach to therapy—too many patients simply did not get better. He raised the problem of the paralysis of analysis with Freud.

Might there not be a deficiency of spirit, asked Binswanger delicately, such that certain people were unable to raise themselves to a level of "spiritual communication" with their analysts? Could this lack of spiritual communication be the thing that stopped people from healing? To Binswanger's surprise, the old man readily acknowledged his point. "Yes," he said, "spirit is everything."

Binswanger thought that Freud must have misunderstood his use of the word *spirit*, perhaps thinking he meant something on the order of "intelligence." But Freud continued on.

"Mankind has always known that it possesses spirit," Freud said. "I had to show that there are also instincts."

When Freud sought to make room for instincts against the background of spirit, he did not anticipate a time when we would forget about spirit altogether. He could not foresee an era when instincts would reign supreme. By the time I was growing up in twentieth-century America, however, spirit already seemed out of reach. Freud's psychology was the accepted language of the mind, challenged only by B. F. Skinner's behaviorism. Those of us who sensed a "deficiency of spirit" were aware only of a feeling of absence, a yearning for something intangible, a sense of emptiness that could not be explained. We did not have words or concepts for what we were missing. Even today, one of the most common questions that I am asked is the meaning of the word *spiritual*. Many people have lost touch with it altogether.

"Anything that takes us beyond the personality," I usually reply. The most important gift that my encounters with Buddhism have given me is access to this spirit that Freud seemed to have taken for granted. Its recovery was of crucial importance to me.

Freud was wrong on one particular point in his conversation with Binswanger: Mankind does not always know that it has spirit—sometimes we forget.

HOW PEOPLE CHANGE

Examples of this forgetting abound, even among those searching for a spiritual life. The split between instincts and spirit comes up in my practice all of the time. A woman named Sally, for instance, called not so long ago seeking advice from me. I had seen her for a single session in consultation months before, and we had talked about a variety of therapeutic and spiritual issues. She was suspicious of the role of psychiatric medications in today's culture. It seemed like some kind of brave new world to have mood-altering drugs so readily available. But Sally wondered if there might not be a medicine that could help her. She had been plagued with chronic feelings of anxiety and depression for much of her adult life, and despite a healthy investment in psychotherapy she still felt that there was something the matter with her.

Sally had been taking a small dose of an antidepressant for several weeks, ten milligrams of Prozac, and she was finding that she felt calmer, less irritable, and, dare she say, *happier*. She was planning on going to a two-week meditation retreat later that month and was wondering whether to stay on her medicine while she was there. Something about taking it while on retreat made her uncomfortable, and that was the reason for her call. "Perhaps I should go more deeply into my problems while I'm away,"

Sally questioned. She worried that the antidepressant would impede that process by making her problems less accessible to her. What did I think?

I was relieved to hear that Sally was feeling better. People who respond well to these antidepressants often have few, if any, side effects. They find instead that they feel restored, healed of the depressive symptoms that they were expending so much of their energy trying to fend off. Less preoccupied with their internal states, they are freer to participate in their own lives, yet they often wonder if they are cheating. "This isn't the real me," they protest. "I'm the tired, cranky, no-good one you remember from a couple of weeks ago." As a psychiatrist, I am often in the position to encourage people to question those identifications with their symptoms. Depressed people think they know themselves, but maybe they only know depression.

Sally's question was interesting not only because of the drug issue but because of her assumptions about what would make her feel better. The notion that we need to go "more deeply" into our problems in order to be healed is a prevalent one, and one that, as a therapist, I am sympathetic toward. Certainly, ignoring the shadow side of our personalities can only lead to what Freud once called "the return of the repressed." Yet it struck me that there was a remnant of American Puritanism implicit in Sally's approach, or at least a Judeo-Christian tendency to divide the self into lower and higher, or better and worse. Her belief that she should go more deeply into her problems reminded me of the Freudian emphasis on the instincts.

When people believe that they *are* their problems, there is often a desire to pick away at the self, as if by doing so they could expose how bad they really are. People think that if they could just admit, or even believe, the awful truth about themselves, they would start to feel better, but feeling bad about oneself seems, in fact, to be a bottomless pit. One never reaches the far end of it. While it usually fails as a strategy, "going more deeply" into our problems can be just another variant on trying to get rid of them altogether, back to a state of imagined original purity like the Garden of Eden. While most therapists would probably deny a religious influence on their thinking, many often collude unconsciously with this mode of thought.

Going more deeply into one's problems is the standard approach of most therapies—and it can indeed lead, at its best, to a kind of sober honesty and humility that gives people a quiet strength of character.

But to go more deeply into our problems is sometimes to go only into what we already know. This approach can also lead, at its worst, to a kind of jaded pessimism about the self, a resigned negativity that verges on self-hatred. I was quite sure that Sally did not have to go *looking* for problems on her retreat. Retreats are difficult enough, even for people who are not depressed. Her unresolved issues would come rushing in to fill every space whether she took her antidepressant or not, but she might have more success in not being sucked in by them with the medicine inside of her. I told her that at this point I felt she needed to come out of her problems, not go into them more deeply, and that the antidepressant would not get in her way in that regard. To be overwhelmed while on retreat would not be useful.

As a therapist influenced by the wisdom of the East, I am confident that there is another direction to move in such situations: away from the problems and into the unknown. Sometimes this fills us with fear. But if we stay with our anxiety, we have a special opportunity to know ourselves more authentically. Buddhism is very clear about how important it is to move in such a direction, and, as such, it is relentlessly optimistic. Rather than going more deeply into our problems, Buddhism teaches us how to disentangle our minds from them. There is, in the Buddhist view, more to the mind than just neurosis. At the heart of all of us is the potential for kindness, generosity, and wisdom.

This is an approach that Western therapy has little experience with, but it is the foundation of Eastern wisdom. The contents of the mental stream are not as important as the consciousness that knows them. The mind softens in meditation through the assumption of a particular mental posture called "bare attention," in which impartial, nonjudgmental awareness is trained on whatever there is to observe. Problems are not distinguished from solutions in this practice; the mind learns how to be with ambiguity while learning to be fully aware.

In my work as a therapist I have found it necessary to bring what I have learned from Buddhism back into the psychological realm. The spirit that

Binswanger noticed ebbing out of the field is essential if true healing is to take place. People who are suffering want to change, but they do not know how. They feel, like Sally, that they have to go into their problems, or somehow get rid of them entirely. They want to analyze, or be analyzed, and they want to love, or be loved. But they do not know that to bring about true healing they have to learn how to see themselves as they truly are.

THE BUDDHIST PERSPECTIVE

"How does your interest in meditation make you different from a conventional therapist," people wonder when they learn of my study of Buddhism. "Do you teach your clients to meditate?" they ask.

For a time I simply dodged the question, repeating a joke that one of my patients relayed to me: "What is the difference between a Buddhist and a non-Buddhist? A non-Buddhist thinks there's a difference."

Buddhism taught me to let go of concepts and opinions and to break down constricting boundaries, not to create a new ideology. Meditation taught me to be with whatever I was doing. It encouraged me to be myself. It taught me to wash the dishes when I was washing the dishes, to walk when I walked, and to play with my children when I played with my children, to be more fully in the moment, in the Now, engaged in the process of being alive. It was not about creating a new form better than the old form.

I like the story of the Zen master whose students were horrified to find him eating his breakfast and reading the paper at the same time. "You taught us to do one thing at a time!" they admonished him, "and now look at you!"

"When eating breakfast and reading the paper, just eat breakfast and read the paper," he shot back.

Meditation taught me to give myself over to my role as a therapist. Like the Zen master, I did not have to look like I was always meditating, but I could try to be as present as possible. When doing therapy, I was just doing therapy. I did not assume that I was different from a non-Buddhist therapist. I certainly did not ordinarily teach my clients to meditate, although if they asked me I would tell them who I thought a good teacher might be.

Yet as I considered the question, I realized that my answer was also a little disingenuous. The positive outlook of Buddhism does guide the way I work as a therapist. It molds my approach from the beginning and affects everything from my goals to my method to my basic orientation. Buddhism was with me as I made my way in psychotherapy, influencing all of my choices as I developed my own style of working.

I was in the rather unique position of learning about Buddhism—both in theory and in practice—before I knew very much about anything else. This was different from the usual mode in our culture, in which Buddhism is encountered as Other, and attempts are made to understand it through the filters of our own systems of knowledge.

Still a college student, I was fairly naive when I first came upon the Buddha's psychology. It did not seem alien to me—in fact, it made much more immediate sense than the first writings on psychoanalysis or behaviorism that I had already studied in my first years at Harvard. While I was interested in becoming a therapist by this time, I did not know much about what it actually entailed. Only after immersing myself in Buddhism did I decide to enter medical school to pursue training as a psychiatrist. My involvement with Buddhism predated the bulk of my education as a psychotherapist.

THE INTRINSIC-REALITY INSTINCT

The core teaching of Buddhism is a psychological one. In his Four Noble Truths, the Buddha analyzed the human condition and taught the vehicle for change. Experience is tinged with a sense of pervasive unsatisfactoriness, he declared, and the cause of this pain is our own clinging or grasping after certainty and security. There are three types of clinging, said the Buddha: for pleasant sensory experiences, for "being," and for "nonbeing." The first needs relatively little explanation, it is equivalent in many ways to the Freudian sexual drive and involves the seeking after sensual gratification, but the second two contain the heart of the Buddhist approach.

From the Buddhist perspective, there is another, more fundamental, instinct than the Freudian ones of sex and aggression. While it is sometimes referred to as "ignorance," it is called the *intrinsic-reality instinct*, the tendency to see a false and absolute identity in people and in things, to falsely conclude they have an intrinsic reality, or essence, at their core. It is the major illness of the human personality, the Buddha realized, to see things as "something" or as "nothing." The ego needs to concretize reality so it can be understood and managed, and this extends to our experience of ourselves as well. We cling to "being," and believe that our selves are absolutely real, that they have self-identity, intrinsic reality; or we swing to the opposite extreme and cling to "nonbeing," seeing ourselves as nothing, empty, and unreal. But both the *something* and the *nothing* are wrong, the Buddha saw; they both precipitate out of our clinging for certainty. Later Buddhist teachers and philosophers developed a "central way" between *something* and *nothing*, and taught methods of training awareness to be able to open-handedly hold or maintain such an approach. It is this teaching that provides a bridge between instinct and spirit, between Freud and Binswanger. It is the intrinsic-reality instinct, the belief in ourselves as somebody or as nobody, which has to be uprooted in order for spirit to be set free.

As I evolved my own style, as every therapist must do, I have come to see how much this core insight of Buddhism influences the way that I work. It gives me a hope and a method for my work that I would not have had otherwise. I know that if I can rest in the "central way", if I can help people find their attachments to being and nonbeing, their own authentic selves—their own *Buddha nature*—will shine through.

This book is, in one sense, a case study about how I came to dwell more easily in awareness, and, as such, I hope it may offer some insight about how others may do the same. This book is also about the traditional Buddhist path of insight, which makes it possible to live in accordance with change, as one's truest self. Living in this way is a potential for all of us that emerges naturally when we see ourselves as we actually are. We can change, it turns out, not by trying to make our problems go away nor by going into them more deeply, but by learning how to be more aware.

ALREADY FREE

I had a visit with an early teacher of mine recently, Ram Dass, at his home
in northern California where he was recovering from a crippling stroke that
he had suffered the year before. Body and spirit were both much in evidence in our meeting. The visit reminded me of how much of my own
search had been inspired by him. The author of *Be Here Now*, and one of the
pivotal figures of the sixties, Ram Dass was engaged in a process of physical rehabilitation and speech therapy designed to bring his body back from
the stroke. While his outward form was altered, his inner one was still very
familiar. He had trouble finding his words at times, but when he did, they
seemed to express his thoughts perfectly. He had not lost any of his inner
vitality or wisdom. He walked the length of his porch with the aid of a
walker and then lowered himself into his wheelchair. I sat beside him on the
porch, gazing into the distance at the leaves of the trees shimmering in the
afternoon breeze. He asked me if I felt I had carved out some new territory
between Buddhism and psychotherapy. "For myself, you mean?" I asked
him, knowing that he tended to be suspicious of the psychotherapeutic
model and of the appropriation of spirituality by therapists. He indicated
this was what he meant, and I, in turn, nodded my assent.

"Do you see them—" Ram Dass began, and then he paused. The breeze
blew through his silence. "Already free," he murmured, as I strained just a
bit to make sure I was hearing him properly. It took me a moment to put
together what he was asking me; it was the only time that afternoon that I
had trouble understanding him.

"Do I see my patients as already free?"

He nodded. He knew the essence of the Buddhist approach. People
come to me seeking something, and I have to know that they are already
free. "They are souls seeking God," he said. "The game is to pretend with
them that they are lost and then help them rediscover their freedom." The
therapeutic relationship is a grown-up version of the child's earliest game
of peek-a-boo.

Ram Dass's insight was pivotal. Our freedom is already present within us,
but we allow it to be obscured by our own clinging. It is as if we are playing

hide-and-seek but we forget midway through that it is a game. We forget we are hiding and feel lost instead. The trick, as Ram Dass understood, is to open up the process of looking so that we can reconnect with the awareness that is already there.

As I sat on the porch in conversation with my old teacher, I touched on all of the contours of my own evolution. My earlier sense of being lost or locked out of myself, yearning for intimacy, my discovery of Buddhism, my relationships with family, spiritual teachers, and therapists, and my processing of these experiences into my work all seemed to be of a piece. Time's inexorable march surrounded us: Ram Dass was in a wheelchair. "Your hair is gray!" he had said as he greeted me, shaking his head and chuckling. There we sat, words and silence intermingling, old friends reminiscing, the warmth of our feelings enlivening the lazy afternoon. "This was like a delicious appetizer," said Ram Dass as I gathered myself to leave.

I was momentarily surprised by his analogy. "An appetizer?" I wondered to myself. I was ready to wrap it up already, preparing to make my departure. It was one of those times that seemed to encapsulate the trajectory of an entire life, and, to me, it felt more like dessert than an hors d'oeuvre. But Ram Dass was catching me in my tendency to seek closure too precipitously. I was all too ready for nonbeing. He might be older and more frail, but he was not saying goodbye. We had just managed to find each other; I did not need to close it down already. I reconsidered my reaction.

An appetizer sounded just fine to me.

PART ONE
THE CENTRAL WAY

I was like a mad child, long lost his old mother,
Never could find her, though she was with him always!
But now it seems I'm about to find that kind old Ama,
Since Big Brother Relativity hints where she hides,
I think, "Yes, yes!"—then, "No, no!"—then, "Could it be, really!"
These various subjects and objects are my Mother's smiling face!
These births, deaths, and changes are my Mother's lying words!
My undeceiving Mother has deceived me!
My only hope of refuge is Big Brother Relativity!

—Jankya Rolway Dorje, *Discovery of Mother Voidness*
(translated by Robert A. F. Thurman)

CHAPTER 1

GOING ON BEING

There is a story that has kept popping up in my work over the years that embodies much of what I have learned about how people change. It is a story that has served a number of different functions as I have wrestled with the sometimes competing worldviews of Buddhism and psychotherapy, but it ultimately points the way toward their integration. It is one of the tales of Nasruddin—a Sufi figure who lived around the thirteenth century, who was an amalgam of wise man and fool. I have sometimes identified with Nasruddin and sometimes been puzzled by him. He has the peculiar gift of acting out our basic confusion and at the same time opening us up to our deeper wisdom.

I first heard this story many years ago from one of my meditation teachers, Joseph Goldstein, who used it as an example of how people search for happiness in inherently fleeting, and therefore unsatisfactory, pleasant feelings. The story is about how friends came upon Nasruddin, searching outside on the ground one night, crawling around on his hands and knees under a lamppost.

"What are you looking for?" they asked him.

"I've lost the key to my house," he replied.

They all got down to help him look, but after a fruitless time of searching, someone thought to ask him where he had lost the key in the first place.

"In the house," Nasruddin answered.

"Then why are you looking on the ground?" he is asked.

"Because there is more light here," Nasruddin replied.

I suppose I must identify with Nasruddin to have quoted this story so often. Searching for my keys is something I can understand. It puts me in touch with a sense of estrangement, of yearning, that I've had quite a bit of in my life, a feeling that I used to equate with an old reggae song by Jimmy Cliff called "Sitting in Limbo."

In my first book I used this parable as a way of talking about people's attachment to psychotherapy and their fears of spirituality. Therapists are used to looking in certain familiar places for the key to people's unhappiness, I maintained. They are like Nasruddin looking on the ground, when they might profit more from looking inside their own homes.

In my next book, I returned to this story obliquely when I described locking myself out of my running car while trying to leave a meditation retreat that I had just finished. I knew I had locked my keys in the car (it was idling away right in front of me, for goodness sake!), but I still felt compelled to look on the ground for them just in case I might somehow be miraculously saved. Being locked out of my car, with it running on without me, seemed like an apt metaphor for something akin to the title of my first book, *Thoughts without a Thinker*. Something like a car without a driver, or, in this case, a driver without his car. Humbled by my own ineptitude, I felt closer to Nasruddin in my second pass through his story. Rather than seeing him simply in his foolish mode, as a stand-in for psychotherapists looking in the wrong place for the key, I felt sympathy for Nasruddin, allied with him searching in vain for what he knew was not there.

But it was not until some time later, when I came upon the same story in someone else's work, that I could appreciate it in yet another way. In a marvelous book entitled *Ambivalent Zen*, Lawrence Shainberg told how this same parable captivated his imagination for ten years. He, too, thought that he understood it. The moral, he concluded, is to look where the light is since darkness is the only threat. But he determined one day to ask his Japanese Zen master (a wonderfully engaging character as described by Shainberg) for his interpretation.

After Shainberg described the story to him, his master appeared to give it no thought, but sometime later the roshi brought it up again.

"So, Larry-san, what's Nasruddin saying?" the Zen master asked.

"I asked you, Roshi."

"Easy," he said. "Looking is the key."[1]

There was something eminently satisfying about this answer; besides having the pithiness that we expect from Zen, it made me look at the entire situation in a fresh way. Shainberg's roshi hit the nail on the head. Nasruddin's activity was not in vain after all; he was demonstrating something more fundamental than initially was apparent. The key was just a pretext for an activity that had its own rationale.

Freud evolved one way of looking; the Buddha discovered another. They had important similarities and distinctive differences, but they were each motivated by the need to find a more authentic way of being, a truer self.

SOMEBODY VS. NOBODY

I had the sense very early of feeling lost and cut off from myself. This feeling motivated my spiritual and psychological search, but it also had the potential to make me feel terrible about myself. In my discovery of Buddhism, I found a method of cutting through the self-estrangement that so bothered me. I found a new way to look at myself.

In the 1970s, there was a saying in Buddhist circles, "You have to be somebody before you can be nobody." This was a popular statement because of how clearly it summed up a very obvious phenomenon. Many of the people who were drawn to Buddhism were attracted by the ideas of "no-self" and "emptiness" that are central to the Buddha's psychology. But these are subtle concepts, difficult to understand correctly; in the Tibetan Buddhist tradition, for example, monks often study the scriptures that explain them for years and years before even starting to meditate. In the West, people who were suffering from alienation or from spiritual and psychological distress often mistook the Buddhist descriptions for an affirmation of their *psychological* emptiness. "You have to be somebody before you can be nobody" was a way of telling them that their psychological work of raising self-esteem or creating an integrated or cohesive self had to precede efforts at seeing through the ego. In many cases, this was indeed sound advice; but the categorization of people into the two categories of "some-body" and "nobody" created another set of misunderstandings.

When the Buddha taught, he asserted both "somebody" and "nobody" were mistakes; that the true vision of who and what we are involves look-ing without resorting to the instinct of intrinsic reality. "Somebody" was the equivalent of clinging to being, while "nobody" was the same as cling-ing to nonbeing. In either case, the mind's need for certainty was short-changing reality. The correct view, the Buddha perceived, lies somewhere in between. The self-centered attitude is as much of a problem as the self-abnegating one. We can be proud or empty; in either case the problem lies in our sense of self-certainty.

Rather than blaming my upbringing, or other people, or instincts beyond my control, this view offered an approach that taught me to work first and foremost with my own *reactions* to things. When I thought I was somebody I reacted one way, and when I thought I was nobody I reacted another. In either case I was obscuring my own awareness. Removing these obstacles opened me to myself—not as something or nothing, but as a unique, sin-gular, and relational process. I learned to live more in the moment—not putting up a false front and not focusing only on what was expected of me, but in touch with a more spontaneous, creative, and responsive self. Like Nasruddin, I was indeed searching for something. Learning to be, instead of react, turned out to be the key.

Meditation was the vehicle that opened me up to myself, but psy-chotherapy, in the right hands, has similar potential. It was actually through my own therapy and my own studies of Western psychoanalytic thought that I began to understand what meditation made possible. As compelling as the language of Buddhism was for me, I needed to figure things out in Western language as well. Psychotherapy came after meditation in my life, but it reinforced what meditation had shown me. Change did not come from trying to get rid of my problems or from going into them more deeply. It came from accepting what was true about myself and working from there. In exposing my chronic ways of reacting, psychotherapy showed me where my blind spots were. It sometimes took the interaction with another per-son to reveal them to me, but the results were similar to what I had glimpsed from sitting on the cushion: As I learned to question my own identifications, I came to be able to live more fully in the moment, and I felt closer to who I really was.

THE HERE-AND-NOW

My own experiences in psychotherapy were with two Gestalt therapists in rapid succession, one in Boston when I was going to medical school, and one in New York where I moved after my internship. They were friends, the former having been a student of the latter, and my work with one merged into my work with the other. I used to ask my Boston therapist, Michael Vincent Miller, where he had learned his craft. He seemed so adept at using whatever was happening in the moment to show me how anxiety caused me to clamp down on just the quality of self-awareness that the Buddha harnessed in his process of liberation. He used to tell me about his teacher in New York, Isadore From, whom he said had taught him most of what he knew about Gestalt.

Gestalt therapy is an adaptation of psychoanalysis that focuses on the "here-and-now" of the therapy encounter rather than a probing of the past. Many of its ideas have influenced mainstream analytic thought by now, but its great expertise is in working with the nuts and bolts of the personal relationship between therapist and patient. As developed most precisely in the writings of the sociologist-turned-therapist Paul Goodman in the 1950s, Gestalt therapy focuses on the deficits in ego-functioning that keep a person estranged from both herself and other people. While the emphasis on "ego" at first glance appears to be the antithesis of Buddhism, in actuality this approach requires a kind of meditation in action.

In Gestalt therapy the natural or satisfying thing is thought to be "contact"—contact between one person and another, between an individual and her environment, or a person and his inner world. Life unfolds in a series of meetings between an individual and his surroundings, which take place at what Gestalt therapy has called the "contact-boundary" of experience. This meeting is sometimes disturbed and sometimes not. When it is disturbed, it is usually through some kind of chronic inhibition or restriction that the person puts on herself without knowing that she is doing so. The therapist's job is to slow things down enough so that it becomes obvious how someone is getting in her own way, in order that she may learn to lift the restriction, if she so desires.

When I was in treatment my therapist often stopped me in mid-stream to ask me to repeat what I was saying and *tell it to him*. I was always offended to be interrupted, and often felt he was not really listening if he could stop me like that, but over time I came to respect what he was after. Talking to him directly made me more anxious but revealed how difficult it was to relate openly. The point of stopping and doing it over again was to discover *how* I got in my own way, how I shut myself down without being aware. Once I could see what I was doing to myself, I could start to change. I would not have known how I was avoiding him, or even *that* I was avoiding him, if he had not stopped me to request that I start over; I would have continued to be caught up in my story and restricted by anxiety without knowing that I was so restricted. Whatever I was saying always turned out to be less important than how I was having trouble saying it.

FREEING THE EGO

This is how meditation and therapy began to come together for me. My own therapists were not students of meditation, but this did not stop them from being able to focus on the here-and-now with a precision and discipline that I both admired and envied. They engaged in a way that I was hungry for. Here was a psychotherapy that was not so much a probing of the past as it was a probing of the present. What was getting in the way of my ability to be open, of my ability to communicate, of my presence in the here-and-now? What was stopping me from being myself? Usually, it would turn out to be some notion of how I *should* be, some image of perfection, some protective sense of embarrassment or shame that caused me to react against the way things actually were. These feelings had led to coping strategies that had taken on a life of their own. It was like assuming a posture that becomes so habitual that it is no longer noticed. I had developed ways of dealing with my anxiety that now ran on without me.

When I would speak to Isadore about something that was bothering me, for example, I would often preface it with a phrase such as, "You know, part of me wishes that I could try that again."

"You don't have parts," he would invariably reply, again skipping over the content of whatever I was talking about to focus on the *way* in which I was expressing myself.

At first, this sort of comment made no sense to me. I was not even aware of having prefaced my remarks in such a way. "What are you talking about?" I would wonder. "Did I say anything about having parts?" But gradually I began to see how regularly I made use of this kind of language. My tendency to divide myself up into conflicting "parts" was a sign of a distancing maneuver that I was engaged in with my own self. By saying "part of me," I was subtly pushing away whatever I was feeling, reducing it to a subset or a fraction of myself and endowing it with an absolute identity. In the midst of these subsets I felt unsure and at times unreal. "You are a whole person," my therapist was trying to tell me, "not a fragment of one." Being a whole person did not mean having no inconsistencies, but it did mean being able to take responsibility for all of what I was feeling. I could want things that conflicted with each other, but then it was up to me to reach a conclusion about what to do. Splitting myself into parts that were in conflict with each other did not do anything to further my situation, it only tended to paralyze me.

My chronic ways of reacting to new situations came in patterns that had a history dating from childhood. I tended to read situations for signs of rejection and then close myself up to forestall it. I could reach out, but then withdraw very quickly if I thought I would be disappointed. I was an expert at figuring out what was expected of me and giving people what they wanted, but I did not always acknowledge what *I* wanted. As I began to take possession of myself, exposing those coping mechanisms to the light of awareness, pivotal memories naturally arose that showed where some of that behavior had originated. Anxiety, I discovered, "is a dread of one's own daring."[2] But these insights into my past came from attention to the present; they were inadvertent byproducts of a willingness to examine my own fears of engagement. Their recovery, by themselves, was not what seemed to be healing. They were more like icing on the cake, affirmations of an ability to relate with less fear and reactivity.

I remember once trying to explain the Buddhist view of self to Isadore. In Buddhism, there is said to be no fixed, intrinsic identity; only a flow with no *one* behind it. Isadore had no problem with the Buddhist view. Gestalt therapy also sees the world as a flow; as a continual unfolding, a succession of meeting places at the contact-boundaries of experience. The "ego" is the individual vehicle for carrying out these meetings, but it has no intrinsic identity either. A healthy ego initiates, approaches, makes contact, and dissolves, only to begin the cycle again. A disturbed ego gets in its own way and interferes with healthy contact, perpetuating its own reality at the expense of the interaction. When I was having trouble speaking to Isadore directly, my ego was actually more active than when I learned to relate openly. In those circumstances where my ego did not dissolve, I was left with a sense of deficiency, having failed to accomplish the intimacy or relationship that I was naturally seeking. An ego that gets in its own way never gets to transparency; the result is a person contracted around his own sense of inadequacy. A positive sense of self emerges only when the ego allows itself to melt away.

Therapy showed me, as if under a microscope, how my ego was not free, how it was hung up on feelings of unworthiness that had stymied me for much of my life. By asking me to do such simple things as talk directly, or change my language as I spoke, my therapists put me in a position to stare directly into those deficits, instead of avoiding them. The ego could be undone only by knowing itself. When it did, it was happy to recede. My feelings of lack were windows into my lost potential. When I learned how to take their appearance as an opportunity to make contact instead of an excuse to avoid it, I was well on the way to relief.

GOING ON BEING

In psychotherapy I found an interpersonal parallel to meditation, but it was not until I came across the writings of the British child analyst D. W. Winnicott that I found the *raison d'être* for such an approach. Winnicott had the theory that put together much of my experience for me. He wrote evocatively of what he called a young child's "going on being," by which he meant the uninterrupted flow of authentic self. It was this flow that I recovered, in different ways, from both meditation and psychotherapy. In Winnicott's schema, there is nothing so precious, or even sacred, as the continuity of a person's capacity to go on being. If a young child has too much to deal with (Winnicott's classic examples of early trauma are usually of maternal anxiety or depression), then she is forced into a reactive mode he called a caretaker self that removes her from her own experience, forcing her to cope prematurely with the needs of another. This interrupts the child's own continuity, producing gaps or breaks that Winnicott liked to call "threats of annihilation." Such a child is never given enough room to develop a continuous and integrated sense of herself. She is forced into a reactive mode that "cuts across" her going on being.[3]

I felt an immediate affinity for Winnicott's descriptions. The fragmented sense of myself, in which I was divided into "parts," seemed to be a result of a process much like Winnicott described. I was good at figuring out what was expected of me, at reading the environment for clues, but I had trouble staying with my own experience. Both meditation and psychotherapy returned a mysterious and invigorating essence to my experience, an intangible quality that was both energizing and enlivening. In meditation, I experienced this as joy or rapture, but in my life it felt more like aliveness or vitality.

Winnicott wrote about this essence in a way that tied a good deal of my experience together. He could speak from the perspective of an infant, a child, a parent, or a therapist, and most of what he said was in agreement with a Buddhist understanding. Going on being does not need to connote any fixed entity of self, but it does imply a stream of unimpeded awareness, ever evolving, yet with continuity, uniqueness, and integrity. It carries with it the sense of the unending meeting places of interpersonal experience, convergences that are not blocked by a reactive or contracted ego. Winnicott supported the obvious sense of an ongoing individual presence, but he was suspicious of a self that was too knowable. The known self is a false one, he would assert, consolidated only for the purpose of managing a malignant environment. And the shadow of that false self is disturbing and oppressive negative space: the emptiness and unreality that can seem even more real than life itself.

Going on being implies an intrinsic but elusive process of self-discovery and self-creation, akin to what in Gestalt therapy is called "creative adjustment," in which inherited potential flowers into full expression through the active participation of the individual. In most Buddhist cosmologies, the analogy for this blooming of potential is the lotus flower growing in the shallow muck of a pond. Given the right circumstances, the lotus bursts forth in all of its splendor, just as our minds naturally flower if brought out from the influence of reactivity.

Winnicott's notion of going on being is the Western equivalent of the lotus. As the representation of each individual's potential, going on being implies the capacity to live in a fully aware and creative state unimpeded by constraints or expectations. Winnicott describes such a state throughout his writing, employing imagery not often found in the language of psychoanalysis. He talks of therapists and mothers in the same breath, as benevolent forces with destructive potential. He warns that well-intentioned interpretations in therapy can be intrusive and might frighten people away, just as he warns mothers to let their babies find the nipple, not to just force it into their mouths. Patients have to find their own meaning in the interaction with the therapist, not just be fed interpretations.

PICKING THE LOCK

In Buddhism, the refusal to be caught in self-certainty is equivalent to the greatest insight of all, that of the "emptiness" of things. In the iconography of Buddhism, in fact, this emptiness (or *shunyata*) is also represented by the mother, because they both, in a way, make everything possible. If things have no intrinsic or absolute reality, then everything must be relational. Emptiness is like a web or a matrix that makes one thing dependent on another. Understanding *shunyata* is not a way of negating the reality of things, of withdrawing from the world or claiming that nothing matters. It is not a nothingness or a void. It is a way of reclaiming the sense of going on being that Winnicott extolled. The literal image behind the term of *shunyata* is that of a pregnant womb: empty, nourishing, fertile, and containing the entire world. Its root is in the Sanskrit word *shvi*, meaning "to swell," like a seed or a balloon. Just as Winnicott held up the mother as the exemplar of what the mind is capable of, so do Buddhists see the potential for transforming the mind through the experience of *shunyata*. The mind can become more womblike, not in the classical Freudian way of hysteria, but along the lines of Winnicott's theory, able to encompass the individual's going on being.

I have one more insight into the fable of Nasruddin. It came through a story in a collection of Jack Kornfield's entitled *After the Ecstasy, the Laundry*,[4] a discussion of how people integrate their spiritual understandings in real life. Jack tells of a Muslim man who was put into prison for a crime he did not commit. A friend came to visit and smuggled him a present, a prayer rug. The jailed man was disappointed, he did not want a prayer rug, he wanted a hacksaw or knife or something else that would somehow aid his escape. But after some time he decided to make use of the rug, studying the beautiful and intricate patterns as he did his daily prayers. One day he started to see an interesting design in the carpet, a diagram of the internal mechanism of the lock to his cell. He picked the lock and was free. As Nasruddin foretold, looking was indeed the key.

Recovering the ability to go on being is like seeing the blueprint in the rug. We feel cut off, locked out, estranged, or imprisoned, and we yearn for release. We have all kinds of ideas about what will heal, about what we have to do to change. But the major obstacle is that we do not know how to look at ourselves as process. We can only imagine somebody or nobody. Yet neither of these options will bring us to freedom: both imprison us.

Like the man in the jail staring at the floor of his cell, everything we need is right in front of us. We don't have to change to awaken, we have only to awaken to change.

PART TWO
THE ILLNESS OF BEING SOMEBODY

The grandeur of real art . . . is to rediscover, grasp again and lay before us that reality from which we live so far removed and from which we become more and more separated as the formal knowledge which we substitute for it grows in thickness and imperviousness—that reality which there is grave danger we might die without ever having known and yet which is simply our life, life as it really is, life disclosed at last and made clear. . . .

—Marcel Proust, *In Search of Lost Time*

CHAPTER 2

THE FREEDOM OF RESTRAINT

As I look back at who I was before Buddhism, I can see that the idea of freedom, like spirit, was alien to me. I had more of a sense of lack than freedom, a feeling that what I needed was just out of reach. A serious child who was vaguely aware of missing something, I could never be sure of what it was I was missing. It was only later that I began to appreciate that I was missing myself.

My own search started early. When I was about six years old, I began to dig. It was a little strange of me, somewhat out of character for a boy who liked books and baseball and riding his bike. But I was determined. I set to work in the backyard of my Hamden, Connecticut, home ostensibly searching for arrowheads. Like Freud, who collected antiquities and often compared the excavation of the unconscious to an archaeological dig, I was intrigued by the idea of an earlier people inhabiting the ground upon which I rested. I had a wooden shovel with a metal handle and I got blisters on my fingers from using it. I do not know how long my digging actually went on, but the hole got pretty big. Even at the age of six, I had the sense of having lost something.

When I was eleven, we went to live in England for a year, and during the long spring holiday from school I went with my classmates on a ten-day exchange to Vichy, a town in south-central France. We were separated from each other and given to French families for safekeeping. My family spoke no English, gave me an attic room at the top of the stairs with a porcelain washbasin on a wooden nightstand, and fed me *café au lait* and bread and jam for breakfast. They had no running water and took me once every few days to the local public baths to wash. I was completely lost, twice removed from everything I had ever known. I cried exhaustively, as I could never remember crying, not from homesickness but from total alienation. Without language to back me up, I had nothing to fall back on. I started to feel better when I spotted the show *Mr. Ed* on French TV, dubbed but still recognizable. "A horse is a horse, of course, of course, but no one can talk to a horse of course."

I was back on familiar ground. After a few more days, the French language began to make sense to me. I could even understand the unsuspecting extended family at their Sunday farmhouse get-together when they talked and chuckled about me.

Yet that sense of utter aloneness made a big impression on me. As a therapist I would expect that it reminded me of an earlier time in my life that I could not specifically remember but that must have felt similar. I thought about it with the French word *oublier*, meaning "to forget." I liked the rounded sound of that word, with its connotation of "oops" and the sense of something somersaulting out of view. *Oublier*. I had lost touch with something, but I did not know what it was. Mr. Ed was a good stand-in, but I was never going to be satisfied with a talking horse.

RECOVERING THE SPIRIT

Freud felt that the religious impulse originates in the helplessness and anxiety of childhood, and perhaps my story bears this out. Yet I have come to believe that his interpretation is only partially true. The spiritual impulse seems also to be one of moving toward something, an unlocking of a more complete expression of potential. Disciplines like meditation train the mind to permit this natural unfolding instead of interfering with it. In and of themselves they offer a way of being that is often sacrificed early in childhood, when the needs of the environment take precedence over the needs of the individual. In this view the spiritual impulse has its origin in the coping strategies of early childhood, for it is those strategies, necessary as they may have been, that choke off or obscure an inherent openness or creativity. Recovery of spirit involves learning how to restrain those very coping strategies that once helped us to survive.

My search continued. The next year I returned to America and started at a new school. A precocious boy in my seventh-grade class, who by the following year had his own apartment in downtown New Haven, started a club of which I became an enthusiastic member. It was called the Tuli Kupferberg Fan Club, named for a member of a newly constituted East Village rock band called The Fugs. We had stamps made that said "The Tuli Kupferberg Fan Club," and we pressed them all over our copies of *The Yearling* and *Red Badge of Courage*. The Fugs, who were led by the poet Ed Sanders, had a song that I especially liked, with a chorus that went something like, "Monday, nothing, Tuesday, nothing, Wednesday, Thursday, nothing. Friday, nothing, Saturday, nothing, Sunday, nothing, nothing." It had other verses, too, of much the same character, and had the poet Allen Ginsberg sitting in and playing a droning instrument called a harmonium. "Ginsberg, nothing, Sanders, nothing, Averell Harriman, nothing," they sang, and I had a jolt of recognition. Was this what I was missing? Nothing?

Several years later the Tuli Kupferberg Fan Club transformed itself into the Eddie Brinkman Fan Club. Eddie Brinkman was a journeyman shortstop for the Washington Senators baseball team, a player with a lifetime batting average of about .230 (not very good) who was known, if he was known at all, for his defense. We chose him to follow (I assumed) because no one else had ever heard of him. There was something about celebrating the anonymous that appealed to us.

As I look back, I can see the links to Buddhism that I was not aware of then. The "nothing" song of The Fugs was directly inspired by Zen Buddhism's Heart Sutra (No eyes, no ears, no nose, no mouth . . . no suffering, no release from suffering), which the Beat poets, of whom The Fugs were an outgrowth, already embraced. The song at first appeared to be nothing more than typical adolescent nay-saying, redolent of the bothersome emptiness I was vulnerable to, but there was a spirit of something hopeful in it as well. Like the Heart Sutra, the verses conveyed an understanding of the limitations of identity, the sense that the name of something is not the same as the experience of it. The fear that I had felt in France when the underpinnings of language were pulled out from under me could be suspended in the emptiness of which The Fugs sang. The song spoke to me, I am sure, because it affirmed my own feelings of psychological emptiness while holding out the possibility of some kind of transformation. Maybe emptiness was nothing, too? There was spirit and celebration in The Fugs' rendition—a sense of hope poking through the void. It made me feel less alone.

In a similar way, our celebration of the anonymous shortstop bore at least some relationship to the Buddhist notion that strivings for celebrity, or identity, are ultimately misdirected. The Buddha's teachings are not about building up the self but about seeing through it, going in a different direction entirely. Freud's attempts to excavate the self also meant probing beneath the surface of things, upsetting conventional notions of social identity. Perhaps digging up the backyard at the age of six can be construed as an attempt to head in this other direction, I cannot be sure. But I do know that as I learned to look inside, the Buddha's *Dharma*, or teachings, began to come alive for me.

EXPLORING THE SELF

As I got older, it was desire that first drew me to the Buddha's Dharma—desire and dissatisfaction. In my first days at Harvard I met an energetic and pretty young woman, a dancer from Westchester, whom I dreamed about right away and whose high school boyfriend was going to the same small college in Arizona that my high school girlfriend had left for. I believed in destiny and asked her what courses she was going to take. She told me *Humanities 11: Introduction to World Religions* (HUM 11), meeting Monday, Wednesday, and Friday mornings. It met a bit early in the morning for my sybaritic tastes, but I signed up anyway, even though it would never have occurred to me to take such a course on my own.

In the most ancient Buddhist temples dating from the first few hundred years after the Buddha, now overgrown and abandoned in India, there are carvings of beautiful bare-breasted dancers called *apsarases* etched into columns that frame the outside of temple complexes. These dancers, celestial nymphs, are often depicted with their heads cocked slightly to one side and one leg bent and resting in a triangle against the other, similar to what in yoga is called tree pose. They seem to usher the disciples toward the center of the *stupa*, where the Buddha is often represented as a wheel or a tree or an empty seat. (These temples date from a time before the familiar, Greek-inspired Buddha image had emerged. In those days it was customary to represent the Buddha only by symbols—an empty seat, a pillar of fire, a tree, or a pair of footprints—signifying that he had gone beyond form.) My dancer friend was like an *apsaras*. Despite the fact that my crush lasted only a couple of weeks, she led me, unwittingly, to a fountain. In quick succession that year we read the holy books of Hinduism, Taoism, and Buddhism: the *Bhagavad Gita*, the *Tao Te Ching*, and the *Dhammapada*. The wisdom of the East was upon me.

"*To know that you do not know is the best*," said the *Tao Te Ching*, in a verse that sent that same shiver of recognition through me as did the earlier voice of The Fugs. It was the perfect counterweight to all of the clamor for knowledge and recognition that I was surrounded by at the time, and it led me forward, toward the Dharma.

> To pretend to know when you do not know is a disease.
> Only when one recognizes this disease as a disease can one be free from the
>   disease.
> The sage is free from the disease.
> Because he recognizes this disease to be disease, he is free from it.[5]

Again and again in these verses from India and China I found intimations of an awareness that superceded our everyday, language-based one.

"*The Tao that can be told of is not the eternal Tao*," I read in the famous first chapter of the *Tao Te Ching*. "*The name that can be named is not the eternal name*."

I loved the idea of learning about nonlearning, in the same way that I had decided in high school that I would be a therapist some day because it sounded like work that was not really work. There was a rebellious streak in me that was dissatisfied with the other available options.

The next year I took a course in psychophysiology. Its subject matter was the mind-body connection, states of consciousness, biofeedback, and the relationship of the nervous system to mood and thought. There were lectures given in an auditorium by a professor, but most of the teaching took place in smaller classes led by graduate students. The fellow who was teaching my section, a young man named Daniel Goleman, had a mop of curly dark hair and was wearing purple bell-bottoms made of wide-wale corduroy on the day I first walked into his classroom. I liked his pants. He was just back from India where he had been researching traditional meditation techniques, and he still had the aura of the subcontinent about him. I could almost smell the incense. My immediate feeling upon meeting him was that I wanted whatever he had: not just the look, but the understanding. It was Danny who told me about Naropa Institute, a school being organized by the Tibetan Buddhist pioneer, Chögyam Trungpa.

"Some friends of mine are going to be teaching in Colorado this summer," he mentioned to me casually one morning in a Xerox store in North Cambridge, where I was meeting him on some early reconnaissance for my thesis. He was getting ready to return to Southeast Asia on a grant, having just completed his Ph.D. in psychology. "You could go out there if you're interested."

I was interested.

TASTING FREEDOM

When I arrived at the Naropa Institute in the summer of 1974, I felt immediately at home. I did not know anyone, but I knew I was in the right place. The course offerings of this Buddhist summer school were not just theoretical, they were almost all experiential. I was thrown into situations where the spiritual disciplines of the Eastern world were opened up for me. I was amazed at how simple and repetitive they all were. I took a class in the Chinese art of t'ai chi and spent an hour every day practicing three movements: lifting my hands softly up to my chest, pulling them into my breastbone, and lowering them with my palms facing outward. I took a yoga class in which I raised my hands over my head, bent down to touch the floor, and raised myself back up to standing, over and over again. In my first meditation class I learned how to notice the breath coming in and out of my nostrils while repeating the word "in" on the inspiration and "out" on the expiration. I went to a regular *kirtan*, or devotional singing group, in which we repeated the words "Sri Ram, Jai Ram" in a call and response with the leader for hours at a time. I wanted to learn to play a set of Indian drums called the *tabla* but was only allowed to practice one movement with the thumb and forefinger of my right hand. I even took a meditation-inspired dance class, in which we walked up and down a forty-foot line on the floor for the duration of each period, making only the smallest of variations in our movements.

Through all of this, my mind was incredulous. "This is so stupid," I would think to myself, while at the same time finding it difficult to keep my focus on the tasks at hand. "What could be more boring?" I wondered, as I kept thinking of an old Kurt Weill song that contains the line, "Is that all there is to love?" I had traveled halfway across the country, and I was not prepared for this kind of simplicity. It was not what I had been trained for. No matter how many books I had read, or facts I had mastered, or problems I had solved, I could not get a leg up on these deceptively simple routines that were being thrown at me wherever I turned. I came seeking freedom, filled with the exuberance of my youth and the inspiration of the sixties, and all I found was restraint. Years later, when watching the movie *The Karate Kid* with my children, I felt a moment of kinship with the young karate student in the film who is forced, in his first lesson with his Japanese master, to spend his time washing cars, practicing the same circular polishing movement throughout a seemingly endless day. "This isn't karate," he complains, as he suffers through an interminably long, hot day in the sun.

The lesson of this first confrontation with spiritual discipline was a profound one for me. Far from being a dead end, these repetitive, boring, and stupid practices held the key to the freedom that I was pursuing but could not understand. All of these disciplines threw me back into my own mind; they brought up a host of reactions that I did not want to acknowledge. I was not so patient and accepting as I would have liked to have thought. I was impatient, judgmental, and obsessively lost in repetitive thoughts. I could think about the same things over and over again in lieu of being in the moment. The spiritual practices all required me to pay attention to the present, and, if this was not possible, to whatever prevented me from doing so.

This was inordinately difficult for me. "Look how hard it is for you to do even a simple task clearly," the practices seemed to taunt. "Look how distracted your mind is, how it jumps all over the place, how it won't leave you alone." I could not even breathe in and out without finding myself washed up on some marshy out-cropping of my own creation. My struggles gave new meaning to the psychoanalytic term "projection." It went from an abstract concept about shaping the world in our own reflection to a concrete description of how self-created obstacles kept tripping me up. My mind was constantly manifesting new and more jagged projections that caught me as I rushed by. No sooner would I dislodge myself from one than I would find myself wrapped around another. It started to feel very crowded in my head.

It was also very crowded at the summer institute, which was named after an Indian saint of the eleventh century who had an important role in establishing Buddhism in Tibet. The teachers to whom I gravitated were all Americans newly returned from Asia who, each in his or her own way, had a similar message. They all taught me to watch my mind. "Do not be distracted by your own reactions," they said. "Awareness can grow if you cut through your habitual responses to things." They did not really expect me to be able to be in the moment, I soon realized. The repetitive practices were all ways of working with reactivity so that I could unlock my mind.

Luckily, there were three of these American interpreters whose words resonated for me, each of whom put his own individual spin on things, and each of whom I was privileged to get to know over the next few years. Ram Dass, Joseph Goldstein, and Jack Kornfield had all studied a form of Buddhist meditation called *vipassana* while in Asia. *Vipassana* means "insight," and the distinguishing characteristic of this form of meditation is that it is meant to provide insight into the true nature of self. It is a way of undercutting the instinctive tendency to see intrinsic reality in persons or in things.

I was majoring in psychology at the time, needed a topic for my senior thesis, and was determined to find it that summer amid the Buddhist teachings that I was gravitating toward. The intellectual kernel within the alternative culture was attractive to me then, as now. "Insight" seemed like a promising place to begin. It was, after all, what psychotherapy was supposed to promote. Wasn't this an important link right away? Didn't both psychotherapy and meditation heal by means of insight? Enticed by the idea, I began to narrow my focus. I did not need five disciplines, I concluded, I only needed one. With some reluctance I let my study of t'ai chi, yoga, tabla, and movement become subordinate to my pursuit of meditation. I was getting the message, I felt. Now I wanted to know the messengers.

The most important messenger was the Buddha, of course. Teaching in India during the same time period as Socrates in ancient Greece, the Buddha was one of the world's first great psychologists. He was able to articulate a positive psychology, one that did not just pathologize but held out potential for the human mind. When the Buddha spoke about the benefits of insight, he described a freedom very different from what I had been taught was possible, and yet he was clear about how to get there. Freedom could only come from restraint, he declared, restraint of the mind's tendency to grasp or push away, to reify things or deny their reality. In my beginning exposure to actual meditation practice, I could see that he knew what he was talking about. My mind did chronically hold on or push away, but it was possible to do neither, if only very briefly. Those first moments of acceptance were quite extraordinary. They filled me with hope.

UNCOVERING THE TRUE MIND

"We are what we think, having become what we thought," begins the Buddhist collection of verse called the *Dhammapada*, and it is possible, the Buddha declared, to change what we become by changing how we think. "A disciplined mind is the road to Nirvana," the *Dhammapada* repeats several times. I read over a particular chapter in this work many times, trying to make sense of the Buddha's teachings. The chapter was entitled, very simply, "Mind," and it seemed to contain the essence of his thought. The state of my mind was my own responsibility, it seemed to say. I include it here, in its entirety:

MIND

Like an archer an arrow,
the wise man steadies his trembling mind,
*   a fickle and restless weapon.*

Flapping like a fish thrown on dry ground,
it trembles all day, struggling
*   to escape from the snares of Mara the tempter.*

The mind is restless.
To control it is good.
A disciplined mind is the road to Nirvana.

Look to your mind, wise man;
look to it well—it is subtle, invisible, treacherous.
A disciplined mind is the road to Nirvana.

Swift, single, nebulous,
it sits in the cave of the heart.
Who conquers it, frees himself from the slavery of death.

No point calling him wise
whose mind is unsteady,
who is not serene,
who does not know the Dhamma.

Call him wise
whose mind is calm,
whose senses are controlled,
who is unaffected by good and evil,
who is wakeful.

He knows the body for what it is, a frail jar;
he makes his mind firm like a fortress.

He attacks Mara with the weapon of wisdom,
he guards what he conquers jealously.

It is not long before the body,
  bereft of breath and feeling,
lies on the ground, poor thing,
    like a burnt-out faggot.

No hate can hurt, no foe can harm,
as hurts and harms a mind ill disciplined.

Neither father, mother, nor relative can help
as helps a mind that is well disciplined.[6]

I was suspicious of the notion of nirvana that the verse pointed to, but it was abundantly clear to me that the description of my mind as undisciplined was all too appropriate. I loved the idea of mind as something both treacherous and potentially serene. A fickle and restless weapon, but a weapon nonetheless. If these verses, written some time before 250 BC, could be so accurate about my undisciplined mind, perhaps they were right about the possibility of change. I knew it required a leap of faith, but I was willing to experiment. If nirvana was the antidote for this rushing and trembling mind, I thought, I'll take two and call in the morning.

I was disappointed, of course, to find that nirvana was not a pill I could take to feel better. By all accounts, it was not a thing at all, and no one could even show me what it was. But this was far from my primary concern. As I began to explore the Buddha's teachings, one thing became overwhelmingly clear. I did not know myself very well at all. Fortunately, the teachers in the chaotic Naropa environment were willing to help me get started.

CHAPTER 3

THE EASING OF IDENTITY

I n the Buddha's Four Noble Truths, he suggested that our lives are colored by a pervasive feeling of unsatisfactoriness. He used the word *dukkha* to describe this feeling and said that it was one of the fundamental characteristics of psychological experience. We want what we can't have and don't want what we do have; we want more of what we like and less of what we don't like. We are always a little bit hungry, or a little bit defensive, anticipating the slipping away of that which we have worked so hard to achieve. Behind every suffering, Buddhist teachers say, is the desire for things to be different. This attempt to control or manage what cannot be changed interferes with our going on being. We worry about the past and anticipate the future or worry about the future and anticipate the past. Our self-centeredness causes us to create an uneasy relationship with the world in which we try to fend off any threats to our hard-fought security. This sets up an indefensible position; we become like a fortress: a self within a mind within a body that is threatened from all sides. As I discovered in my beginning explorations of meditation, my mind was scurrying about in all directions trying to maintain a semblance of control, but this was exhausting or, in contemporary parlance, highly stressful.

As a therapist I have found that a similar process is at work. The desire for control, in the form of being a helper, is as much of an obstacle to healing another person as it is to healing oneself. It is necessary in therapeutic work to avoid trying to accomplish too much. A provocative British psychoanalyst, W. R. Bion, famously declared that a therapist must be free from memory and desire if he is to be of any use to his patients. To think about the end of a session, to wonder what time it is, even to hope for a cure, is to add an agenda that becomes an interference, because it is sensed as a demand. People are exquisitely sensitive to each other, especially in a stripped-down relationship like a therapeutic one. "If the psychoanalyst has not deliberately divested himself of memory and desire," said Bion in his 1970 classic *Attention and Interpretation*, "the patient can 'feel' this and is dominated by the 'feeling' that he is possessed by and contained in the analyst's state of mind, namely, the state represented by 'desire.'"[7] The therapist's identity as a "helper" is felt as an implicit demand, and the patient is disrupted as a result. Desire becomes an intrusion, and the patient goes into an all-too-familiar reactive mode.

Through my meditation I have seen how openness can contain and transform fear, and how striving interferes with this process. Without quite knowing how it was happening, I found an approach to psychotherapy that puts less of an emphasis on understanding and more of a focus on experiencing than I was ever taught in my formal education. When I first came upon Bion's words, I felt right at home, even though many in the field considered him too difficult to understand, too arcane or even mystical. In his later work, Bion developed a system, or a private symbolic language, to express his belief that the quest for knowledge interferes with the emotional truth of therapy, as the quest for insight interferes with meditation. He called the emotional truth O, and wrote of how premature attempts to understand get in the way of it.

I remember coming upon a description of O in a book by Michael Eigen and being thrilled. I read it aloud to my wife at the dinner table, and we both marveled at the prose. "(The psychoanalyst Marion) Milner speaks of Bion's O as zero, but O is also *Omega*, everythingness and nothingness," writes Eigen. "At times Bion uses O to signal the unknown emotional reality of a session, or of a series of transformations, or of group events, or of the cosmos. O may represent the impact of the Other, the shock of impact that sets off waves of feelings, sensations, presentiments. As we ride these waves we may utter a rapturous 'Oh, Oh!' or an 'Oh-Oh!' of trepidation. O is for the orgasmic element that permeates, charges, and sustains experiencing. O is for One, one God, one cosmos, whose streamings we are. O is a circle, the rounds and rhythms of life, eternal returns and reversals, crisscrossing currents, a geometrical representation of the constructive-containing mind that pulsations explode, the Opening of the O."[8] Rapture? Streamings? Pulsations? Orgasm? This was a psychoanalyst I could trust, and one I wanted to know better.

In another particularly vivid passage, Bion describes the unknowability of reality as follows: "It is impossible to know reality for the same reason that makes it impossible to sing potatoes; they may be grown, or pulled, or eaten, but not sung. Reality has to be 'been': there should be a transitive verb 'to be' expressly for use with the term 'reality.'"[9] In both of these passages, Bion's insights approach those of the Buddha. If the mind can be dislodged from its need to concretize reality, something transformative can happen. It is faith, concluded Bion, that permits this kind of being. It is the kind of faith that allows us to jump off a high diving board with the knowledge that we will hit water and not earth. My meditative explorations inculcated me with this kind of faith, but my psychotherapeutic ones have confirmed it. Having learned to jump into my own reality, I am no longer shy about jumping into another's. But it is Buddhism, with its emphasis on the Eightfold Path, that has taught me how not to be an interference in my own right.

THE EIGHTFOLD PATH

As the Buddha articulated the rest of his Four Noble Truths (craving or clinging as the cause of dukkha, nirvana as release from it), he elaborated what became known as the Eightfold Path to enlightenment. These were his directions to nirvana, his description of the dimensions of our lives that require discipline or restraint. They were his means of purifying the mind, of making it lofty, straight, and without obstructions. They were his method of shaping the mind so that it could remain composed in the midst of ceaseless change. They were also his way of training us to deal with three fundamental realities of existence, realities that he called *dukkha* (or unsatisfactoriness), *anicca* (or impermanence), and *anatta* (or insubstantiality).

While there are eight aspects to the Buddha's Path (Right Understanding, Right Thought, Right Speech, Right Action, Right Livelihood, Right

Effort, Right Mindfulness, and Right Concentration), the eight are often grouped into three overarching categories: Right View (encompassing Understanding and Thought), Right Relationship (consisting of Speech, Action, and Livelihood), and Right Meditation (Effort, Mindfulness, and Concentration).

The three teachers whom I met when I first discovered Buddhism each had a particular emphasis that came to correspond, in my mind, with one of the three aspects of the Buddha's Eightfold Path. Ram Dass, with his background in psychology and his ability to make the traditional wisdom of India intelligible to the Western mind, represented Right View. Jack Kornfield, whose years of solitary retreat in a Thai monastery were balanced by an emergent need for family and community, taught the essentials of Right Relationship. And Joseph Goldstein, whose command of classical Buddhist psychology was enhanced by his devotion to intensive meditation, was the embodiment of Right Meditation. All three were newly returned from Asia, where each had developed a relationship with an elder teacher who had guided and inspired him. I was as curious about these relationships as I was about the teachings, sensing the therapeutic nature of those encounters. In their own idiosyncratic ways, these three teachers made the Buddha's wisdom come alive for me. I was fortunate to become their student while at the same time getting to know them personally.

LOOSENING THE BONDS OF IDENTITY

The most well-known of the three was Ram Dass, who had once been named Richard Alpert. When I first met him he was teaching the *Bhagavad Gita* at Naropa, a Hindu mythological epic about devotion and duty, but his lectures were peppered with his own emerging understanding of the principles of Buddhism. Ram Dass hardly needed the platform of the *Bhagavad Gita* to teach from, however. His own story was already operatic in scope and mythic in proportion. We would sit and listen to him for hours, soaking up his humor as he recounted the by now familiar details of his own pilgrimage. Ram Dass's message was "You are not who you think you are." He undercut as many manifestations of the false, caretaker self as he could find.

He had already changed identities several times in his life, evolving from a materialistic, ambitious young professor into an apostle for psychedelia and then to a spiritual teacher. In addressing his own narcissism, he made clear how possible it was to detach from the needs of the ego.

After a successful beginning as an academic psychologist at Harvard, a terrain that was all too familiar to me at the time, the ambitious Dr. Alpert dove, with his colleague Timothy Leary, into the uncharted terrain of research on the psychedelic drug LSD. After several years of increasing confrontation with the academic community and public exposure of their personal explorations, Alpert was dismissed from his position. (The man who fired him, Dr. David McClelland, the chairman of the psychology department at the time, was a professor of mine when I was at Harvard who was rumored to still be close to Ram Dass. He taught courses on Human Motivation and managed to make no references to Ram Dass in his lectures, much to our disappointment.) Released from his academic moorings, Alpert set out for India in 1967, intrigued by the connections he and Leary had already noticed between their psychedelic experiences and Asian spiritual texts like the *Tibetan Book of the Dead*. He had gone as far as he could with LSD, Alpert decided; now he wanted to find someone who knew something of the realms of consciousness that the drug had opened up for him.

After driving all the way to Nepal in a state-of-the-art, $7,000 Land Rover, accumulating beautiful objects but frustrated in his quest for a realized master, Alpert eventually stumbled upon an elderly and irascible Hindu guru in India known as Maharaj-ji, or Neem Karoli Baba. Teasing Alpert from the start, Maharaj-ji grabbed hold of his heart by suddenly making reference to the death of Alpert's mother. "You were out under the stars last night," he said to him in Hindi at their first meeting. "You were thinking about your mother." Alpert was startled, since he had told no one who or what he was thinking about. "She died last year," Maharaj-ji continued. "She got very big in the belly before she died." Alpert's mother had indeed died of a ruptured spleen. Then Maharaj-ji looked Alpert in the eye and said very suddenly in English, "Spleen."

This was the beginning of Alpert's devotion to Maharaj-ji and the point of departure for his transformation into Ram Dass. It provoked a catharsis in which Alpert's rational, thinking mind (his primary defensive tool) was temporarily paralyzed, flooding him with the kinds of buried feelings that signal a return of going on being. But it was not the end of Maharaj-ji's teachings. Still preoccupied with his experiences with LSD, Ram Dass resolved one evening to speak to his guru about the drug. The next morning Maharaj-ji called for him and immediately demanded the "medicine." At first unsure of what Maharaj-ji might mean (he was unused to thinking of the drug as medicine, even though he was carrying it in pill form), Ram Dass soon realized what was being asked of him and ran to his car to fetch the drug. Maharaj-ji held out his hand, demanded three of the pills, popped them in his mouth, and continued on with his day. Nothing seemed to happen to him.

Ram Dass was amazed. Nothing had happened. For Ram Dass at the time, this was the ultimate demonstration of some kind of spiritual attainment. He knew firsthand how powerful the drug could be, and yet here was someone who was totally untouched by it, someone more powerful than LSD. Ram Dass's attachment to the drug was loosened. He came back to America and began to tell his story, but still, somewhere in the back of his mind, he harbored doubts about what he had seen. "Perhaps he hadn't really swallowed them," he thought to himself. "Maybe he just threw them over his shoulder." On his next trip to India, Maharaj-ji called to him again, asking, as if he couldn't quite remember, "Say, did you give me any medicine last time you were in India? Did I take it?"

Ram Dass answered somewhat equivocally, "Well, I think so."

"Oh, did it have any effect on me?"

"No, I don't think so."

"Oh. Go away," Maharaj-ji said. The next morning he called to him again. "You got any more of that medicine?" he asked. "Bring it."

Ram Dass gave him the equivalent of five pills this time. Very slowly, Maharaj-ji took each pill and placed it into his mouth, making sure that he could be seen swallowing each one. Then he began to act agitated. He called for water, questioned Ram Dass about how long the drug would take to act, called for a wristwatch, and then asked, "Will it make me crazy?"

"Probably," said Ram Dass, and Maharaj-ji at that point went down underneath his blanket and came up making all kinds of strange faces. But the joke was on Ram Dass. Maharaj-ji was just playing with him.

At the end of an hour he asked him, "You got anything stronger?" Again, nothing out of the ordinary happened. Ram Dass stayed with Maharaj-ji all day and nothing happened. At one point Maharaj-ji told him that drugs like this were known in India long ago but that knowledge about them was now lost. "It's useful, it's useful, not the true *samadhi*, but it's useful," he said, using a Sanskrit word for meditative attainment to make his point. Later he told the young Westerners who were starting to gather around him in India, "If you're in a cool place and you're quiet and you're feeling much peace and your mind is turned toward God, it's useful." You could have a visit with a holy man in that place, he said. But, he added, you can't stay there, it doesn't last. That's why it's better to become the saint rather than just visit him.[10] Ram Dass was amazed at this display of psychic power. He knew from first-hand experience how the ego could be decimated by LSD. But here was a man who was unfazed by it. Maharaj-ji's ego was so flexible, so transparent, that the drug did not seem to touch him.

This was the first point that Ram Dass was communicating that summer in Boulder. There was a limit to what altered states of consciousness could provide. Getting high was not the same as being free, cautioned this apostle of psychedelia. "Once you get the message, you have to hang up the phone," he would say, in answer to innumerable questions about mind-altering drugs. There was something called *sadhana*, one's own spiritual work, that required diligence, commitment, honesty, and responsibility. Sadhana required working with our own minds, our own hearts, our thoughts, feelings, relationships, emotions, and physical selves. All of the stuff of daily life could be, as he put it, "grist for the mill" of awakening.

For me, Ram Dass was like Moses. Already in his 40s, with a long graying beard and flowing white robes, he seemed like an elder statesman to my young eyes. And he had talked to God in the form of Maharaj-ji. Pointing the way to a new kind of freedom, he made me feel as if my wanderings in the desert might come to a close. LSD was not exactly the golden calf, but we did need to do something other than just worship at the altar of altered states. If we wanted to end our suffering, we had to do a more subtle and far-reaching thing. We had to discover our true natures.

Ram Dass never hid too much of his personal drama from us. His sexual cravings, the illness and death of his father, his despair over the recent death of Maharaj-ji, his own attachments to being smart or right or in control all figured into his teachings. While he did not claim to have completed his quest, he was willing to share the fruits of his journey, and for a twenty-year-old college student like myself who was just getting oriented, this was very useful.

"You are not who you think you are," Ram Dass repeated over and over again, each time throwing my mind into confusion. Thinking was what I did best. How could I know myself if whatever I thought was wrong? There is a kind of knowing that is beyond thought, suggested Ram Dass, that has to do with being, as opposed to doing. He even titled his best-selling book *Be Here Now*. Maharaj-ji had been a living example of this kind of being: a transformative example. Insight erupts out of this kind of being, Ram Dass implied. It does not come from thinking, it comes from learning how to restrain the thinking mind. For someone like me, raised in the backyards of academia and vaguely dissatisfied with the worldview of scientific materialism, this idea of something beyond the scope of the rational mind was both unsettling and enticing. I knew I was good at learning, but I was not so sure how good I could be at unlearning.

RELEASING ATTACHMENTS

Ram Dass told a story that I enjoyed a great deal. It was about his first Zen Buddhist retreat, called a *sesshin*, which had taken place in a Benedictine monastery under the tutelage of a Zen master named Sasaki Roshi. A number of other well-known spiritual teachers were in attendance, among them the Hindu teacher Swami Satchidananda, the writer and Taoist scholar Alan Watts, the Sufi leader Pir Vilayat Khan, and Brother David, a Christian monk. It was a spiritual retreat, but not without competition. Ram Dass was given the *koan* "How do you know your Buddha nature through the sound of a cricket?" Although he knew that he was not supposed to think his way to the answer, he nevertheless spent most of his time composing the perfect response. In his interview he cupped his hand to his ear in imitation of the Tibetan saint Milarepa, who is always portrayed in that pose, listening to the sounds of the universe. "Here I was a Jewish Hindu in a Catholic monastery giving a Tibetan answer to a Japanese koan," laughed Ram Dass. "I was really just delighted with my own cuteness."

The roshi looked at Ram Dass for a minute and then rang his bell to dismiss him. "Sixty percent!" Sasaki cried as he nodded goodbye. As someone who had always measured myself by the grades I achieved, I could appreciate the power of the Zen master's response. I would never want to get a sixty percent!

Ram Dass did not want to either, yet he could appreciate the humor of his predicament. "It caught me perfectly in my middle-class, achievement-oriented identity," Ram Dass told us.[11] He had attacked the koan the way he had learned to figure out a multiple-choice exam, but this was not the route to freedom. Sasaki had deftly shown him where he was attached, and Ram Dass could now pass that information along to us. As I listened to him tell these kinds of stories, I could feel him tugging at my own version of this identity. Right Thought did not mean cleverness, he was saying; it meant the ability to tolerate uncertainty. Even intelligence could be an obstacle to being.

As I listened to Ram Dass that summer, I began to get a sense of what he meant by "discovering where we are attached." Attachment was a difficult word for me, because it had a double meaning. I was alone at the time, in search of love and meaning, and anxious about my ability to be in relationships. In some sense attachment was what I was seeking. But Ram Dass was using the word in another way. Attachment, for him, was what kept him closed off, pursuing his own small-minded and habitual agenda. It was what perpetuated his unrest. Attachment was what Maharaj-ji and Sasaki Roshi were probing, trying to release Ram Dass from the tyranny of his identity.

I could see Ram Dass struggling with his attachment to getting high and to being smart, and I could understand how those attachments restricted his ability to be open. I became interested in what my attachments might be, and I began to question who I thought I was. This was an important starting place for me in my quest for insight. Insight meant discovering where

I was attached and making it conscious, thereby giving me some measure of choice in the matter. This understanding opened up a feeling for another word used frequently in spiritual circles: Space. Seeing my attachments gave me a feeling of space.

Just as my thoughts were all too often running on without my conscious participation, so did my personality seem to operate mostly on autopilot. It was not exactly unconscious, because I could tune in to it at will, but it was habitual and therefore mostly unaware. It was almost as if my identity, like my thoughts, was happening just to the side of me, just outside my grasp. Following Ram Dass's example, I began to see that a mind without obstructions meant a personality whose attachments were brought fully into awareness. Freud's dictum to make the unconscious conscious could be more profitably rephrased as bringing what is unaware into awareness. Dehabituate the habitual attachments. Restrain the habitual impulses. Rather than being compelled to react in a certain way, this approach permitted me a sense of spaciousness within myself, a spaciousness in which I was more conscious of who I used to be and more open to who I might become.

THE BUDDHIST WAY OF CHANGE

As I got to know Ram Dass over the years, I heard him reflect often on the transformative potential of this approach. His psychologist mind was able to put language on the more mystifying events of the spiritual search. As always, his candor and humor poked holes in my own tendency to idealize or romanticize what I learned. "Through all the years of my practice," he would say, "from psychotherapy, from psychedelics, from meditation and yoga, I have never gotten rid of a single neurosis. They are all still there. But they have gone from being huge scary monsters to delightful little schmoos. I see one coming along and I say, 'Oh, there you are again. I remember you. Tricky little thing, aren't you?'"

This insight of Ram Dass's is pivotal. In our desire for freedom, we imagine that we have to eliminate unwanted aspects of ourselves. But the Buddha's psychology does not support such an approach. Change happens naturally as we open to truth. The more we bring our attachments into awareness, the freer we become, not because we eliminate the attachments, but because we learn to identify more with awareness than with clinging. Using our capacity for consciousness, we can change perspective on ourselves, giving a sense of space where once there was only habit. Discipline means restraining the habitual movement of the mind, so that instead of blind impulse there can be clear comprehension.

In the quest to understand where unsatisfactoriness comes from, we are often inclined to search for causes or people to blame. Ram Dass was the first to demonstrate to me the benefits of an alternative approach. This became the cornerstone of my understanding, that the search for causes has to lead eventually back to the individual. Although traumatic and terrible things may have occurred, it is the individual's mind that perpetuates the suffering, and this mind can be trained to change. As long as we are struggling *against* the feeling, hoping to eliminate it by getting high or being cured, we are still attached. We can relieve unsatisfactoriness only by sharpening our focus and changing our perspective.

Yet this was not the end of Ram Dass's message. He also presented his own transformation in the context of his relationship with Maharaj-ji. His spiritual work was not all internal but had taken place through the intervention of another. Maharaj-ji had pulled Ram Dass into a relationship that had shattered his models for what one could expect from such encounters. He had shown him another way of being, and had let him taste it for himself. This was the more subtle of Ram Dass's teachings. For all of his emphasis on meditation and self-examination, his own transformation had taken place in the context of a relationship with an elderly man.

Years later, as I sat with Ram Dass on his porch, he surprised me by asking questions about my former psychotherapist, Isadore From. "We both needed those relationships," he said with a smile. It was a bit of a shock to hear him comparing my therapist to his guru; I thought he would have kept Maharaj-ji in a special category. But I knew at once what he was saying. The wise, cranky, but loving figure who could both cut through and appreciate us was a blessing, whether it came in the form of an Indian *rishi* or a New York psychotherapist. When it comes to going on being, the spiritual and the psychological have quite a bit of overlap.

CHAPTER 4

MINDFULNESS OF MIND

While Ram Dass extolled the freedom that comes from letting go of identity, there was another teacher at Naropa who showed me how to use awareness to loosen my identifications. Joseph Goldstein taught meditation the way a Japanese artist folds origami paper, with exquisite attention to every detail and a simultaneous appreciation for the whole. I remember my first feelings of awe as I listened to him teaching mindfulness of breathing in his class. Here was a twenty-nine-year-old American, newly returned from seven years in India, who did not seem the least bit exotic. His instructions were so clear that my internal protests of "I can't do this" or "This isn't for me" simply crumbled. Joseph had a way of making meditation accessible, of dealing with every impediment thoughtfully and skillfully. His enthusiasm was such that when he first discovered how to meditate in Asia, he invited his friends to come over to watch him do it. When they demurred, he professed astonishment at their disinterest. He had that same enthusiasm at Naropa, except that he was now able to use words to convey his experience, inspiring his students to discover their own.

I was somewhat intimidated by Joseph's formidable intelligence but determined nonetheless to question him about where his knowledge derived from. I went to visit him in his apartment and was surprised to find it full of people. There were at least five or six reading, talking on the phone, cooking, or just hanging out. They were friends from India, he indicated casually, other Westerners who had been studying in Bodh Gaya, the tiny village in the north of India where the historical Buddha was enlightened under the bodhi tree. India was the land of the *schmatta*, he would sometimes laugh, using an old Yiddish word for a piece of cloth, and these fellow meditators seemed to bear out this impression. They would come to his class wrapped in rough shawls of homespun Indian *khadi*, or cotton, looking very self-contained as they sat motionless in meditation. They seemed just as self-possessed in his apartment, joking and bantering with each other. I was expecting a little privacy for my first meeting, but it was not forthcoming. Yet Joseph welcomed me into his communal space, making a bit of room for us to chat.

I wanted to find out something that I did not know how to articulate. Joseph's instructions for meditation were simple and practical, but there was something deceptive, and challenging, in his simplicity. A deep reservoir of psychological material surfaced periodically in his teachings. He talked of "mind" as if it were a Chinese box, or a tangerine, that he could take apart and put back together at will, carefully examining each section, or "mental factor," the way a jeweler pores over a precious stone. He talked of a self that does not exist, of a freedom that comes from balancing effort with surrender, of a joy that was inherent to the mind but outside the range of everyday experience. What he promised was tantalizing, yet elusive. The freedom he evoked seemed very possible one moment and completely out of reach in the next. But he never seemed to tire in his attempts to convey the mind's possibilities.

THE CENTRAL IMPORTANCE OF MINDFULNESS

Joseph did not ignore the meditation techniques of concentration or one-pointedness, in which the mind is fixed on a central object like the breath, a prayer, or a candle flame. Indeed, he explained the importance of this kind of nondistractability, or *samadhi*, in terms of the Eightfold Path's Right Concentration; but his emphasis was definitely on something else. Concentration meditations were well known in the Buddha's day, and the Buddha mastered them without finding the key to liberation. Joseph made much of something called mindfulness, the ability to note, moment-to-moment, what was happening in the mind or body when it was happening, without holding on to it and without pushing it away. Practicing

mindfulness meant carefully noting to oneself whatever was most promi-
nent in one's experience through the construction of what seemed to me a
somewhat artificial witness, or third party, in the mind. How could this
simple act of "noting" bring about the kinds of psychological changes that
he was promising? What did mindfulness, which seemed like so much of an
effort (and a rather obsessional one at that), have to do with freedom or joy?

The answers to these questions seemed to revolve around stories of monkeys. Perhaps his fondness for simian metaphors had to do with all the
years he spent in India. The mind, he would say, is like a monkey in the way
it restlessly jumps from object to object. I was not too familiar with monkey habits, but I could understand what he was getting at. Incessant thinking makes us tired and uncomfortable; our minds are untrained, distracted,
and driven by habit. The first task in meditation is to discipline the mind
by noting all of its reactions. In India one way a monkey is trained is by
pounding a big stick into the earth and attaching a long rope to it, at the
far end of which is fastened the monkey. Given a lot of rope, the monkey
is free to jump around a good deal, but at a certain point, if the animal
strays too far, he is always jerked back by the tether. After enough time of
being pulled back like this, the monkey eventually settles down and stays
within the radius of the rope. Concentration on the breath is like the stick
in the ground; it is the central object around which we structure our meditations. Mindfulness is like the long rope. When our minds are wandering,
it jerks us back into the present moment.

I could see from my beginning attempts at meditation that this analogy
was a good one. Concentrating attention on my breath gave me a certain
fleeting peace of mind, a semblance of security or calm. But my mind would
not stay concentrated for long. I could go for extended periods lost in
thought, even when I appeared to be meditating. Eventually I would notice
that my attention had wandered, and I would bring myself back, for an
instant, to whatever was happening. This function of remembering was a
beginning bit of mindfulness, repeatedly waking me up to the present. Meditation, I came to see, was not so much about keeping focused as it was about
bringing my mind back when I noticed that it had wandered. I could not
bring it back before I noticed, but once I became aware of my inattention, I

could begin anew. The great mystery was in how I became aware of my wandering mind in the first place. What was it that woke me up in the midst of a daydream? This, Joseph told me, was the rope of mindfulness. As I practiced, it would get stronger, and my monkey mind would start to settle down.

I did not know it at the time, but this method of teaching was completely synchronous with Winnicott's notion of going on being. In noticing the mind's reactivity, I was learning to work with my caretaker self. All the habits and patterns that I had evolved to protect myself came out in meditation. The simple act of trying to rest my awareness on the breath allowed me to see them in vivid color. As I became less reactive to my own reactivity, I started to peer into myself more. This, in turn, encouraged me to listen to Joseph more closely.

He invoked the monkey metaphor in one other way. When monkey hunters in India want to catch their prey, he said, they fashion an ingenious trap made of a hollowed-out coconut shell. This shell is attached to a tree or a stake in the ground, and a bit of sweet food is put inside. A small hole is made in the shell and the trap is left waiting. When an inquisitive monkey smells the food, he reaches in and grabs it. The hole is big enough for a monkey's hand to enter but too small for the clenched fist, clutching the sweets, to pull out. When the hunters come, the monkey becomes frantic but will not open up his fist to let go of the food, even though this simple act would set him free.

Like these monkeys, we cultivate our attachments instead of learning how to let go. Mindfulness is the antidote; it is training in not holding on. Requiring a radical acceptance of whatever was happening, whether I liked it or not, mindfulness offered a means of rising above my own individual cravings. In one sense, our attachments are to pleasant sensory experiences that, like the monkey, we are reluctant to relinquish. But in a deeper sense, there is an even more subtle and pernicious attachment that the monkey story introduced. This is the attachment to self.

UNDERSTANDING NO-SELF

I did not know it at the time, but Joseph's teacher of seven years in India, a Bengali man named Anagarika Munindra, had an encyclopedic knowledge of Buddhist psychology that had filtered directly into Joseph's understanding. Like Ram Dass with Maharaj-ji, Joseph's relationship with Munindra had enabled him to absorb the Dharma. At the heart of Munindra's understanding was the peculiar notion of *anatta*, or no-self, the central psychological idiom of Buddhism. This seemed like the ultimate trick to me, a psychology without a self behind it. In the teachings, the self was like those schmattas that Joseph's friends draped over themselves. It might give comfort sometimes, but we could just as well take it off. Like a snake's worn-out skin, or the food in the monkey's closed fist, this self was insubstantial and could simply be dropped.

I was intrigued, puzzled, curious, and determined to know more. Like many others in his meditation class, I peppered Joseph with questions that began to have a familiar ring. My biggest and most recurring question in those years ran something like this: "If there is no self, then who is meditating right now? If there is no self, then who is watching this process? If there is no self, then whose knees are hurting?" This was not only my recurring question but seemed to be everyone else's question as well. I did my best to come up with new variations: "If there is no self, then who gets enlightened?" Or, "If there is no self, then how is it that I remember what happened to me when I was young?" (In fact I could not remember much of what had happened to me when I was young, but I managed to skirt that issue for a while.)

It turns out that these early questions were not unique to me, nor to my time and place, but have recurred throughout the history of Buddhism. The story goes that the Buddha, right after his enlightenment, despaired of the possibility of communicating his insights. "They go against the stream," he lamented. "If I were to teach this Dharma, the others would not understand me. That will be wearisome to me, that will be tiresome to me . . ." Only after the great Vedic gods came and implored him to teach did he relent. The Buddha's hesitation was both understandable and unjustified. The sheer outrageousness of his discovery fascinated and touched many different cultures over the next twenty-five hundred years, provoking the same mix of disbelief and fascination that I found upon hearing of his insights.

Even in the first few centuries after the Buddha there are records of this. One instance is preserved in the ancient text *The Questions of King Milinda*, in which the Greek King Menander (or Milinda), the military commander of what is now Afghanistan, who invaded and ruled a great swath of northern India, can be overheard questioning the local Buddhist sage Nagasena. Menander ruled his kingdom from Sagala, a city in the foothills of the Himalayas located somewhere near the modern Pakistani region of the Punjab. As heir to the conquering Alexander the Great, he had imposed a Greek social and political structure on his Indian metropolis, but the cultural and spiritual mores remained primarily Buddhist.[12] Intrigued by the wisdom of his subjects, Menander wanted to know more about their beliefs. His questions, which have an eerie resemblance to ones we asked two thousand years later, ultimately led to his conversion to Buddhism. The victorious general yielded to the wisdom of his Buddhist subjects; he was conquered from within. His questions have a particular resonance because they were asked by a Westerner, the product, just as we are, of Greek philosophy and culture. They focused right away on the Buddha's teaching of no-self.

One of the first recorded conversations between the king and Nagasena began with introductions. "How is your reverence known, what is your name?" Milinda asked.

"O king," Nagasena replied, "I am known as Nagasena, my fellow brethren address me as Nagasena, but whether parents give the name Nagasena, or Surasena, or Virasena, or Sihasena, nevertheless, O king, Nagasena and so on is a term, appellation, designation, a mere name, for in this matter the individual does not exist."

Many centuries before the advent of the French deconstructivists, the Buddhist sage Nagasena proclaimed the self as a simulacrum, a mere designation not to be reified through the unnecessary process of identification. "What's in a name," he was saying. "You can call me what you will, but don't think that you know who I am." Like Tuli Kupferberg and The Fugs,

Nagasena took the radical position of "nothing." At Naropa all those years later, Joseph was no less assured in his proclamation of the absence of self. "Empty phenomena rolling on," he would declare, while we struggled to figure out what he was talking about.

King Milinda felt immediately challenged by Nagasena's confrontation and called the surrounding crowd to witness his next questions. "If, reverend Nagasena, the individual does not exist, who then gives you your robes, bowls, dwellings, and medicines necessary for the sick? Who enjoys them? Who keeps the commandments? Who practices meditation? Who realizes Nirvana of great fruit?" Much as we asked Joseph, "If there is no self, then who is sitting here listening?" Milinda asked Nagasena to explain himself. "If there is no individual, then who are you? And if we do not exist, then why bother taking responsibility for anything?"

These are the most common kinds of questions upon hearing of the Buddha's insights. When faced with his refusal to uphold our conventional notions of self, we rush to judgment on the entire question. As Milinda suggested, either you are somebody or you are nobody, but you cannot have it both ways. If the self is not real, then it must not exist at all. If there is not something, there must be nothing. Our eagerness for certainty boxes us in, and we jump from a materialistic view of self to a nihilistic one. But the nihilistic view is still materialistic. It is as easy for the mind to conceive of nothing as it is to conceive of something. What is difficult is to imagine something else.

I had no problem accepting the possibility that my sense of self was flawed. But, like Milinda, I found it difficult to imagine what my true self might look like. I could conceive of being nothing, but I had more difficulty imagining myself as a something that was not something.

In *The Questions of King Milinda*, Nagasena attempts to address this problem by asking the king how he traveled.

"Now," he continued, "did you come on foot, or in a carriage?"

"I did not come on foot, reverend sir, I came in a chariot."

"If your majesty came in a chariot, explain to me what a chariot is," Nagasena replied, zeroing in on what has become a traditional Buddhist symbol of the self. "Can the chariot-pole be the chariot, O king? Is the axle the chariot? Are the wheels, or the frame, or the banner-staff, or the yoke, or the reins, or the goad, the chariot?" To each of these questions the king responded in the negative. "Then, O king, is the chariot all these parts? Well, O king, is the chariot anything else than these?" Again, the king said no. "O king, I ask and ask you, and do not perceive a chariot. Is 'chariot' anything but a mere word? What is a chariot in this matter? Your majesty is uttering a falsehood: there is no chariot. . . . Thus says this King Milinda, that he came in a chariot, but when he is asked, 'If your majesty came in a chariot, explain to me what a chariot is,' he does not produce a chariot; is it a wise thing to approve of this?"

By pointing to something so concrete and obvious as the chariot, Nagasena was making a difficult point. The chariot obviously exists. It is more than a mere word, but it exists only in relationship to its parts. In Buddhist terms, we would say it exists as the designation of its parts. In the Buddhist psychology known as Abhidharma, the self that we take to be real, like the chariot of King Milinda, is a similar kind of vehicle. It has a reality but not the intrinsic one we assume through the process of identification. We can see form (the five sense organs and their objects), feelings, perceptions, mental factors, and consciousness, but we would have a hard time putting our finger on "self." Traditionally referred to as the five *skandhas*, a word that translates as something like "heaps" or "aggregates," these five are continually referred to in Buddhist works. They sometimes run the risk of being turned into miniature selves, as in, "there is no self, but there is form, feeling, perception, etc." But the idea of the skandhas is to convey the ever-shifting, fluid nature of the mind-body continuum. When they come together they create the conditions, or the circumstances, for the appearance of self, as a hologram is created out of light, or a chariot out of its parts.

According to Buddhist psychology, there is something that goes under the term, designation, or name of "self " that is dependent upon the coexistence of its parts. This self is certainly not nothing, but is it the something that we imagine? Can we even be justified in using a noun like "it" to designate it? Our language does not give us too many options; this is a good example of how we are sometimes imprisoned by it. Conventionally, of course, there is the appearance of a self, but upon examination it does not turn out to be what we imagine. "In the strict sense," concluded Nagasena in his conversation with King Milinda, "there is no individual in the matter."[13]

MAKING LIGHT OF IT

This inference, which lies at the heart of the Buddha's teachings, seemed to me at first fairly unimpressive. "So what," I said to myself. "What difference does it make anyway?" I wanted Joseph, in my meeting with him, to explain it to me once and for all, but he just referred me back to my meditation cushion. "Insight grows out of mindfulness," he told me. Although I was feeling a bit suspicious, I decided to give it a try. This led to one of my first surprises in meditation. As I learned to watch my own mind, I began to see how I was continuously creating my sense of self through my thoughts. It was not some elaborate construction, but a simple and reflexive habit. Over and over again, I was repeating the words "I" or "me" to myself. "I don't like that," I would think. "Not for me," I might add. I was always telling myself what I thought.

People talked about an inner dialogue, but I seemed to have more of an inner monologue. "What would it be like if I could stop buying in to all this?" I wondered. This was where Joseph was helpful. He did not encourage me to try to drop the word "I" from my thoughts, for example, as I might have naively attempted. He talked instead of the mind's tendency to identify with its experience, and he was clear that this identification was separate from the experience itself. As I studied Buddhism throughout the years, I found that this approach of Joseph's was replicated in all of the different schools of Buddhism.

The trick in Buddhist meditation is to focus on the feeling of self as it appears, as absence or as presence. In the Tibetan tradition, the best time to find this sense of self is said to be in moments of "injured innocence," when we feel hurt or outraged at the way someone is talking to us or treating us. This is when the self is thought to be most visible to our observing consciousness. It feels so real that we can almost put our finger on it. But the key word here is "almost." Even under these circumstances the self remains elusive. It just cannot be grasped. But the feeling of identification can be perceived as something extra.

This was not something that I could have thought of on my own. Yet it seemed to be true. The skandhas were not abstract concepts; they were descriptions of various forms of identification that create a sense of self. I could identify with my body, my feelings, my perceptions, my thoughts, or my consciousness. But it was possible to observe identification as it happened, or to feel it happening and then to let go of it. I experimented with this in my meditations. It was not so hard to locate the sense of identification, nor was it particularly difficult to release it. Trivial events triggered minor realizations.

At one of my first meditation retreats, for example, the woman sitting next to me, a friend of Joseph's named Kishorri who was wrapped in an Indian schmatta, leaned over to request that I breathe a bit more quietly. Momentarily insulted, I nevertheless tuned in to how I was straining in my efforts to pay attention to my breath. I realized then that if I could just let the breath breathe me, I did not have to be in charge. The same held true for my thoughts and my feelings. Everything carried on just fine without me.

This was a little bit unnerving, like dreams I have had where I could suddenly breathe under water. My identification was like food coloring in water. It did not change the substance of things but completely altered its appearance. "Wait a minute," I would think after suddenly glimpsing how my process continued without me. "How is this possible?" It is a strange feeling not to be needed. But this was unexpectedly liberating: it led me to a lighter touch. Bitten by the Buddha bug, I began to open myself to this possibility in an ongoing way.

These first encounters with Buddhism opened me up in a number of ways. Rather than struggling against my experience by feeling sorry for myself or fearing my insecurities, I now had a stance or a posture, an approach to life that guided me. Relieved of some impinging sense of responsibility for everything, I became much more able to allow experiences to unfold as they did. Less judgmental toward my own emotional responses and less invested in always maintaining control, my interior life became more textured and nuanced as I relaxed my grip and began to feel more at home in my body.

I saw that my feelings arose together with my awareness, but that it was possible to take the me-ness out of those feelings, to make light of them. I sensed this lightness both literally and figuratively, in the buoyant quality of some of my meditations but also in my growing capacity for humor. I did not need to, nor could I, stop my most disturbing feelings from arising, but I could use my observing awareness, my mindfulness, to create a sense of space even around them. Deepening my experience of myself, I felt, at the same time, relieved of a heavy burden. I became more interested in investigation than in control, less sure of myself in some ways but more willing to explore whatever I was experiencing. If fear was only a feeling that I did not have to identify with, what did I have to be frightened of? A cliché, perhaps, but life suddenly seemed much more liveable. I did not think of Buddhism as a religion, but I had discovered faith.

LOOSENING IDENTIFICATION IN THERAPY

In my work as a therapist, these lessons from Buddhism about loosening identification never cease to inspire. They pop up at the oddest times. People turn to therapists with their feelings of injured innocence, hoping to find an echo of reassurance. When feelings are hurt, or when someone has been mistreated, it is important for a therapist to be supportive and to encourage an appropriate response, but it is equally important to shine a light on their patients' self-centeredness, helping them to question their own certainty, so that they may grow. A therapy session with a man named Chuck demonstrates a bit of this philosophy.

At his wedding, Chuck's godmother gave the new couple one bit of advice. "Never go to sleep angry," she warned them. "Make up before the day is done." Chuck thought this was very sensible; it went right along with his study of Eastern philosophy. Greed, hatred, and delusion are the causes of suffering. Why would he and his wife want to feed the fires of such destructive forces? Yet things had not worked out as he had envisioned. Some years into the marriage Chuck and Rachel had fights that never seemed to get resolved, at least not in the way he thought they should. He still believed that they should not go to sleep angry, and as a consequence he would stay up all night processing his rage while his wife slept.

In a session with me several days after their latest argument, Chuck told me what he had been through. He and Rachel had been driving to a friend's party but the printed directions were wrong. Chuck got off at the indicated exit, headed west as he was instructed, but could not find the next landmark. "Why wasn't it there?" he wondered. He snapped at his wife, assuming that she wasn't reading the directions properly. Irritated with his tone, she told him that she was reading them just fine, but she asked him to stop to ask for help. He assured her he would, but then sped past the next gas station. They were late already, and he was convinced he could find the place. It was somewhere on this street. He had passed it the day before, he remembered. Careening about in search of the landmarks indicated in the invitation, he sped in one direction, finally stopping at a neon-lit fast food joint straight from a David Lynch movie. A group of four youths eyed his car. He quickly headed back in the other direction as his wife grew more and more irate.

There is nothing that Chuck hated as much as being yelled at in an automobile. He did not like asking for directions and took pride in his ability to find his way, even when lost. He felt that Rachel did not trust him when she lost her temper like this and routinely took it as a blow to their love when she did. He asked her very calmly to please stop yelling at him, but inside he was seething and indignant. Rachel did not find his forced calm appealing and continued to be vociferously angry with him. He became withdrawn while fantasies of crashing their car began to flower in his brain. He finally stopped for guidance at a local motel, drove to the party, and spent the evening waiting for her to apologize, even after they discovered that their host's printed directions had, in fact, been faulty. Chuck and Rachel danced once, to Aretha Franklin's "Respect." The irony of the lyrics was not lost on him.

My friend Michael Eigen, a New York psychoanalyst who, unlike most of Freud's descendants, is not put off by the pursuit of the sacred, told a story in one of his books[14] about a meditator named Ken who came to him for help with his abusive temper. No matter how many times I read it I am always moved. Throughout my talk with Chuck, flashes of Ken kept breaking through. The case study is entitled "Stillness<—>Storminess," with the double arrows indicating a dynamic relationship between the two states, one that both Ken and Chuck were unwilling to accept.

The heart of the story is Ken's anger and his efforts to use Buddhist meditation to calm it. Anger faded and peacefulness opened in meditation. This was a revelation to Ken, the answer to his prayers. But it was not a peace that could last. Ken still got angry in the midst of family life, much to his dismay. Ken's expectations, for himself and for his family, were too great. He demanded that meditation calm domestic life, and he was disappointed every time conflict broke up his meditative stability, blaming himself or his family. He wanted his family to live by his values, to orient themselves around peace and calm, to make meditation the center of their lives, too. He was outraged by the turmoil of family life and drawn more and more to the simplicity of silent sitting.

"Part of Ken's difficulty," writes Eigen, "was his hidden wish to control his family (perhaps life itself) with one mood. He was not content to enjoy calm, then pass into tumult of real living. He wished to rule the latter by the former. An unconscious severity structured his tranquility. Meditation centered him, yet masked a tyrannical demand that life not be life, his wife not be his wife, his child not be his child."

The tyrannical demand that his wife not be his wife. I talked to Chuck about that. He wanted an apology from her, and he could not believe that she would withhold it. *An unconscious severity structured his tranquility.* What about what his godmother had said? Why could Rachel never say she was sorry? "Her punishment did not fit my crime," he repeated to me several times. "Why can you not just let go?" she insisted, in knowing reference to his years of meditation practice.

I thought back to a lecture I had just given. I was speaking about "injured innocence," about those times when you are falsely accused and you think to yourself, "I didn't do that!" The self-instinct is most visible at such moments, and they are thought by Tibetan teachers to be wonderful opportunities to zero in on the self that upon examination turns out to have no intrinsic reality.

A young woman raised her hand and told me she was troubled by this concept. Could it not be used to justify being a victim of abuse? Wasn't it just a kind of masochism? It was a tricky point, I conceded. The ego is necessary to defend against abuse; what I was talking about was more subtle and took place in the natural give and take of most relationships. I could see that Chuck was in a similar position to that woman at my lecture. He felt that he had to stand up for himself and could not use the situation to zero in on his own self-cherishing.

In Michael Eigen's article, he probed Ken's relationship to anger and his devotion to stillness. Ken was not just trying to quiet his own mind, he was endeavoring to silence a chaotic early environment. "In time he realized that he tried to get from meditation the calm he never got from his parents. In part, he used meditation to calm his parents (in unconscious fantasy), as well as himself. Meditation was a way of creating calm parents, calm self." But meditation frustrated Ken in its failure to transform his life. He wanted too much from it, and he began to hate what could not be changed. Instead of using meditation to move between states of storminess and stillness, to let go of one as the other took hold, he tried to use meditation to dominate life. He needed therapy to teach him how to move between states with awareness and flexibility.

Chuck was very like Ken in his relationship to anger. He had a formula for how things were supposed to go. If he and Rachel had a fight, they should be able to process it. He would try to admit his faults, but his wife should be able to, as well. If she was going to get so angry with him, she should at least be able to apologize. But Rachel did not like to talk about such things. She got mad, but when it was over it was over. She did not like all of Chuck's rules. I read Chuck a passage from Jack Kornfield's new book, *After the Ecstasy, the Laundry*, a vivid description of the challenges of incorporating a spiritual awakening into the chaos of everyday life. "What ecstasy?" Chuck murmured, still feeling sorry for himself. Jack quoted seventy-five-year-old Sufi master Pir Vilayat Khan as saying that even the most enlightened teachers he knew in India would have a hard time in America in the face of a spouse, two cars, a house, three kids, a job, insurance, and taxes. Chuck nodded his head silently.

Chuck had difficulty allowing the fight to disappear by itself. He kept wanting that apology. Several nights later when going to sleep, he turned his back to Rachel but was surprised as she nestled against him. Almost against his will, he moved into her softness and warmth. She felt good, and he momentarily appreciated her gesture. Some of his anger melted. I quoted one more story from Jack's book to Chuck, this one about Zen master Shun-ryu Suzuki Roshi of the San Francisco Zen Center. A student asked him, "You tell us to just sit when we sit, just eat when we eat, but can a Zen master just be angry in the same way?"

"Like a thunderstorm when it passes?" Suzuki Roshi responded. "*Ahh*, I wish I could do that."

To no end: you will never find so much as a trace, not even the tiniest, of the mind. The banner of its sovereignty is precisely this: its not being there. No one can ever claim to have grasped it. It is like a dazzle on water: you can follow it, but however far you go toward it, it will always move the same distance away.

—Roberto Calasso, *Ka: Stories of the Mind and Gods of India*

The witness to all this instability, the watcher, seems to be the only stable thing. When you realize this, you begin the most difficult effort that a human being can make, or so it is said. This is the effort that the Buddha successfully made; it is how he became enlightened. You turn the witness on the witness. You become like a dog chasing its own tail. Because you are the self you feel like a unity, but when you look back for that solid unity of self you don't find anything. You then notice that you're still feeling some sense of solid self. Then you look back at what you're still feeling, and you start to spin like a whirling dervish inside the center of your mind. It's very tiring and strenuous. Just looking and looking back becomes a twirling, and then that twirling effort becomes what is called the diamond cutter.

—Robert A. F. Thurman, *Circling the Sacred Mountain*

Meditation made me aware, not only of how entrenched my identity was, but of how precarious it could be. My thoughts were in one place, and my experience was in another. My thinking seemed to have a life of its own, creating a fractured feeling in which I was separated not only from the external world but also from myself. When I started to meditate, I found I could sit for an entire hour without noticing anything going on around me, because I was so taken up with my own thoughts. It was not until I took my meditation practice to another level that I began to break through. I remember this starting to shift early one morning when I went on my first two-week silent retreat.

Having met each other that summer at Naropa, Jack Kornfield and Joseph Goldstein began to teach together in rented facilities around the United States. They taught in northern California and then later that fall in western Massachusetts, at a retreat that I was able to insinuate myself into. School was in session, but nobody missed me much. The practice (as it was often called) had an enormous power for me. It was simple but ever challenging. In alternating silent periods of sixty minutes of sitting and thirty minutes of walking, the task was to keep the attention in the present moment, through awareness of body, feelings, mind, and states of mind. The first few days were a struggle; I was tired, bored, anxious, ambitious, and full of self-doubt. But I was also motivated, and I followed directions as best I could under the circumstances. As I relaxed into the impossibility of the task, several days into my retreat, things began to change. The shift was most apparent in those moments between the official meditation periods, when my effort was less strained and my mind more naturally at ease.

RECOVERING AWE

I remember coming outside one early morning and squatting down to feel the early morning sun on the front porch of the New England seminary we were renting. The sensation of warmth on my skin on those cool fall mornings held my attention and opened my other senses. With my eyes closed, resting against the building wall, I began to listen to the birds whistling in the country air. The notes stretched out all around me, points of sound erupting like raindrops splashing in a vast sea, playing off of each other and off of the silence that separated them. My attention was gathered, not distracted, in those moments, and the world opened itself to me.

There was a recovery involved in this listening, a recovery of what is sometimes called celebration, or magic, or awe. In psychodynamic language, it was a recovery of going on being. No longer endeavoring to manage my environment, I began to feel invigorated, to find a balance, to permit a feeling of connection with the spontaneity of the natural world and with my own inner nature. My awareness became more kinesthetic and .affectively dense—richer, deeper, and, in a curious way, more personal. I felt more grounded, even as I was floating in the sounds of the birds, more rooted in a way of experiencing that felt both entirely new and completely familiar. Surrounded by a landscape of sound, I began to open simultaneously to a landscape of feeling. This allowed me to continue my work on another level. Just as I was learning to accept my thoughts but not be run by them, I could attempt the same in my feeling life. In simultaneously taking possession of myself while disidentifying with the content, I could glimpse a new possibility for my being.

A NEW FOUNDATION FOR THE SELF

Normally we experience the world through the filter of our minds. I do not mean our brains, for of course our brains are involved in the apperception of reality, and I do not mean our minds in the Buddhist sense. I mean the thinking mind, the talking mind, the mind that is language-based and has developed categories and words for raw experiences. In psychoanalytic language, this filter is called the secondary process. It is a way of thinking that gradually emerges as a child matures, the hallmark of successful cognitive development. Its development is essential for us to make our way in the world. We need to think, talk, and maneuver, to communicate with each other and with ourselves, and to do such things we need to make use of the rational, logical, symbolic, and verbal modes that the secondary process represents. Yet, all too often, this new ability gets put to defensive uses. The child of a depressed mother learns to distract her with his accomplishments. The child of an unreliable father becomes the parent in the house. Our minds become reactive, and we feel estranged from ourselves as a result; locked out of our own houses, we are in need of the key to return.

What I found in meditation was that there is another modality besides the secondary process. It is different from what in psychoanalysis is usually called the primary process, that unstructured time of dream or fantasy in which images, feelings, associations, and intuitions achieve dominance in the mental stream. In meditation, there is a kind of focused alertness or relaxed watchfulness that has a peaceful quality which the Buddha described as sweet. It is one of the first things to emerge in practice.

As I relaxed into the sounds of the birds and the warmth of the sun on the porch of the retreat, I had a corresponding deepening in my meditation. A qualified shift took place in my mind. Instead of chasing thoughts or being spun around by them, I found myself in new territory. I could feel my mind settling down and becoming clearer and brighter. I do not mean this metaphorically, I mean it literally. I could feel my mind becoming more attuned. My heart leapt at this lightness, and I felt a pervasive sense of having found myself. According to the traditional schema of Buddhist psychology, I had stumbled upon what is called "access concentration," an advanced beginner's stage of meditation where the mind has the first taste of calm. Certain qualities of mind, called the "factors of absorption," get turned up at this stage.

This was very interesting to me. There was no doubt that I was having some sort of spiritual experience, but it also felt like such a psychological one. My self did not disappear—far from it—but I did feel enriched. Something was definitely changing. No longer thinking all the time, I felt more alive in my self. I looked to the Buddhist literature for clarification about what was happening.

I read how difficult it was for a mind bothered by the "five hindrances" to achieve any kind of peace or stability, and my first several days of intensive meditation had certainly borne this out. Lust, aversion, sloth and torpor (an archaic but evocative way of talking about fatigue), worry, and doubt were never far from my mind, and I could appreciate what I copied out of an ancient text called the *Visuddhimagga*, or *Path of Purification*, about the pernicious influence of these hindrances.

"The mind affected through lust by greed for varied objective fields does not become concentrated on an object consisting in unity, or being overwhelmed by lust, it does not enter on the way to abandoning the sense-desire element. When pestered by ill-will toward an object, it does not occur uninterruptedly. When overcome by stiffness and torpor, it is unwieldy. When seized by agitation and worry, it is unquiet and buzzes about. When stricken by uncertainty, it fails to mount the way to accomplish the attainment of absorption."[15]

I could appreciate all the references to being bothered by flying insects. Summers in Maine had developed in me a real antipathy to mosquitoes, but now I could see that my own mind could be just as bothersome. Pestered, stricken, or seized, "unquiet and buzzing about" was a kind way to describe what those first few days felt like. I was used to these states of mind, if disturbed by them, but I was not prepared for what came next. The factors of absorption snuck up on me. My first few days of diligent practice involved the strengthening of rather innocuous and little-used mental qualities, to the point where they began to anchor and structure my awareness, permitting a level of concentration that was unusual for its clarity and onepointedness. Identified as "initial and sustained attention, rapture, joy, and concentration," these five factors of absorption were like mosquito repellent—they drove away the five hindrances.

Initial attention is what first grabs your awareness when you notice some-thing you are interested in, while sustained attention keeps you focused on it. Rapture and joy are of different grades, like maple syrup or honey; as concentration improves, they get progressively more refined and subtle. It is interesting that in the Buddhist schema, where qualities of mind are mostly divided into those that are skillful and those that are unskillful, these factors of absorption are all said to be neutral. They can be used for both positive and negative purposes. Japanese kamikaze pilots in World War II, for instance, were trained by Zen masters to develop their powers of con-centration in preparation for their suicide missions.

ACCESS CONCENTRATION

In our regular lives we stumble into states of deepened concentration under the spell of physical exertion, music, dance, sexual relations, or pleasant sensory experiences like eating or touch. One of my most profound absorptive states occurred in a little restaurant off of the Piazza de Cam-piori in Rome upon first tasting a simple dish of ravioli with shavings of white truffles one fall. The flavor was so fresh, light, and piquant that I was in awe, completely stopped in my tracks. Savoring the taste, I chewed each mouthful thoroughly while my eyes watered slightly with joy. The proprietor of the trattoria noticed my reaction and came over to me with-out a word, laying one hefty arm across my shoulders and patting my back reassuringly.

But there were no truffles to propel me into absorption on this first retreat; the food was hearty but nothing I would ever reminisce about. And the state of concentration was more lasting than that of the trattoria; it stretched out over time. Hour-long sittings that the day before were ago-nizing were now serene. My mind was not buzzing about, restless or unquiet; there was nothing pestering me. I had the strange sensation of my center of gravity shifting from my brain to my chest. My mind was quiet, but my heart was alive. Light flickered behind my closed eyelids. I might have said that I was filled with love, because that is a phrase that comes readily to my mind, but that is not entirely accurate. I did not really feel like a container. It was more like I was emitting love. I had a sense of myself shining.

In the Buddhist cartography this state of access concentration is like the first clearing in a long hike after a particularly uncomfortable trek through dense underbrush or fly-infested swamps. The temptation is just to rest a while. But in addition to being a clearing, it is also a fork in the road. There are two ways to go on such a trek. One is to continue on the path of concentration, refining absorption such that the grosser elements of joy and bliss give way to a profound equanimity. This is the path of the yogis who are known for their meditative attainments—but it is also the path that the Buddha had to go beyond in order to achieve his final awakening.

The other path involves balancing concentration with mindfulness. This is what is described in an important text called the Satipatthana Sutta, Foundations of Mindfulness (sati). Instead of allowing awareness to narrow on a single object, you widen the focus, now relatively undisturbed by the five hindrances, and begin to observe all of the reactions of body and mind. Known as the path of wisdom, only this kind of self-observation loosens arrogance and conceit. In the first path the attention is progressively restrained and focused, while in the second it is brought under control but then opened up again.

This cartography was helpful to my understanding, if a little dry. From an objective standpoint, the Buddhist psychology texts described in a profusion of detail how the mind changed through meditation, how it was restructured by concentration and mindfulness. But what was missing in these particular texts was the kind of language that I came to discover in psychoanalysis, language that could describe why these changes were so personally moving. This is why Winnicott's descriptions of going on being were so powerful for me when I came upon them years later. He articulated a process that I had seen in my own experience. The disciplining of my mind through meditation had opened up a positive sense of myself, countering an already established tendency toward unworthiness or self-hate. As I found out, the Buddha's own life followed a similar path.

THE DANGER OF SELF-NEGATION

The rough outline of the Buddha's life story was familiar to me. A provincial prince, he was raised by his overprotective father to never see old age, illness, or death. Renouncing his family and privilege at the age of twenty-nine, he became an ascetic, wandering through the forests of northern India in search of his freedom. Sitting under a tree in what is now the village of Bodh Gaya, after exhausting all of the spiritual disciplines of his time, he awoke to the truth of emptiness. But his process of awakening was more complicated than I had initially imagined. There was a pivotal event hidden within his years of renunciation that had all kinds of psychological implications. There, in that critical period after forsaking all that was dear to him but before his awakening under the bodhi tree, was a little-known vignette about a childhood memory that was the turning point in his life. This event also involved a recovery and an enrichment of the self, and it set the stage for his ultimate realization. That his memory had psychodynamic implications is undeniable. It came just at his point of maximum vulnerability, as he was attempting, with all of his might, to subdue himself through penance and starvation.

The Buddha-to-be, Gotama of the Sakya clan, left his wife, newborn son, palace, and kingdom and struck out on his own, pursuing the available spiritual practices of his culture. This was a big step, but it was not a radical one. This was the traditional modality of the spiritual seeker in ancient India, and there were many such seekers. Gotama found several well-known teachers and perfected a variety of ascetic practices, but, unable to penetrate the riddle of his own being, he grew increasingly frustrated. His renunciation became stronger and stronger. Like a modern-day anorectic, Gotama pushed the limit of his own endurance and refused even the least possible nourishment. With five companions looking on in anticipation of the fruits of his penance, he struggled to reach beyond the limits of his mind and body. As the Buddha later recounted it,

"I thought: 'Suppose I take very little food, say, a handful each time, whether it is bean soup or lentil soup or pea soup?' I did so. And as I did so my body reached a state of extreme emaciation; my limbs became like the jointed segments of vine stems or bamboo stems, because of eating so little . . . my ribs jutted out as gaunt as the crazy rafters of an old roofless barn; the gleam of my eyes sunk far down in their sockets looked like the gleam of water sunk far down in a deep well. . . . If I made water or evacuated my bowels, I fell over on my face there. If I tried to ease my body by rubbing my limbs with my hands, the hair, rotted at its roots, fell away from my body as I rubbed, because of eating so little."[16]

The Buddha was on the brink of self-eradication. In trying to subdue himself, and the restless passions he had already identified as part of his problem, he succumbed to the use of force, beating himself into submission, as the ascetics of his time counseled. He was trying to go deeply into his problems, with an eye toward getting rid of them once and for all. The Buddha, it seems, was once headed down a path of self-abuse. He was human, too, subject to the same kinds of psychic pressures that afflict most of us, and he seemed to have felt as unworthy as any late-twentieth-century initiate into psychotherapy. While this approach of self-subjugation may sound alien at first, it is not actually so far removed from the kinds of strategies that many people still employ. The self-starvation of anorexia and the incessant self-criticism of the judging mind are ascetic practices in their own right. Unworthiness takes many forms, but at its heart is a confusion about one's own promise.

The Buddha was close to destroying himself when he suddenly took his attention in another direction. In one of those moments like that in which a chronic smoker finally decides to quit his habit, the Buddha saw that he had reached his limit. At his most forlorn point, he started to question himself, making a remarkable turnaround that established joy as the platform upon which the entire promise of enlightenment is based.

"I thought, 'Whenever a monk or brahman has felt . . . painful, racking, piercing feeling due to striving, it can equal this but not exceed it. But by this grueling penance I have attained no distinction higher than the human state, worthy of the noble one's knowledge and vision. Might there be another way to enlightenment?'"

This thought—"Might there be another way to enlightenment?"— proved to be critical. It opened up the memory that at first must have seemed irrelevant to the Buddha's question. I can imagine him trying to brush it away, a disturbing thought echoing from the canyons of child-hood, of little interest to this starving forest ascetic. But like an associa-tion in psychotherapy, the memory had a hidden meaning. The Buddha did not ignore it at all. Trusting in his own psychic process, he gave it his full attention and probed for what it might reveal. The memory centered, as did his subsequent enlightenment, around a tree. In the midst of self-punishment, Gotama remembered a time of wholeness under a tree. An episode of pleasure tugged at his mind.

"I thought of a time when my Sakyan father was working and I was sit-ting in the cool shade of a rose-apple tree: quite secluded from sensual desires, secluded from unwholesome things, I had entered upon and abode in the first meditation, which is accompanied by thinking and exploring, with happiness and pleasure born of seclusion."

Reflecting upon his time under the rose-apple tree watching his father work, the Buddha remembered a simple pleasure that had sprung from his own state of mind, one that he compared to the fruits of concentration meditation. Under the canopy of the protective arbor and his father's benevolent but noninterfering presence, the young child experienced a taste of the joy that is born out of relaxed contemplation, the pleasure that was his being. In the midst of his ascetic practices, he had lost touch with that simple happiness. Suddenly it came flooding back to him. "Might that be the way to enlightenment?" the incredulous Buddha thought to himself. "Then, following up that memory, there came the recognition that this was the way to enlightenment." In recognizing that it was indeed the way, he continued his investigation.

What happened next is, for me, the most crucial. The Buddha noticed that there was something scary about this pleasure that appeared out of nowhere. "Why am I afraid of such pleasure?" he wondered. He said only one thing in reply, leaving it to us to fill in the rest. This is the Buddha at his most psy-chologically astute. In reading the passage, I can almost see his mind work-ing. He remembered his pleasure and in the next breath recognized his fear of it. As the Jungians would say, he saw his own shadow. And then he was quick to analyze. "It is pleasure that has nothing to do with sensual desires and unwholesome things," he thought; that is what is causing so much fear.

THE DIRECTION OF RELIEF

This is a fascinating realization but difficult to understand. Why should this be scary? Why should a pleasure that jumps out of nowhere, not dependent on sensual desires, be frightening? Perhaps because it challenges our identity as someone who is lost, hungry, cut-off, deprived, bereft, searching, or in need of (as we say in psychodynamic language) an object. It challenges our assumptions about the direction of relief. The pleasure feels too great, too undeserved, too blinding. Yet this, as the Buddha intuited, is the direction of enlightenment. This reminded me of what I had been told the great fourteenth-century Tibetan teacher Tsongkhapa, the founder of the Dalai Lama's school of Buddhism, purportedly said at the moment of his enlightenment: "It's exactly the opposite of what I expected!"

The Buddha, after a moment's reflection, saw through his fear. A pleasure that did not depend on the gratification of desire was a pleasure inherent to what is. If happiness was inherent to what is, then why push reality away? Why engage in these self-punishing exercises at all? Sensual grasping was not the route to happiness, but neither was its suppression. In a flash the Buddha renounced renunciation and set out to nourish his body. The first recorded instance of self-analysis had done its work.

"I am not afraid of such pleasure, for it has nothing to do with sensual desires and unwholesome things," he reflected. "It is not possible to attain that pleasure with a body so excessively emaciated. Suppose I ate some solid food—some boiled rice and bread."

It is interesting, in the life of the Buddha, to see what this memory unleashed. First of all, the five ascetics accompanying him could not make heads or tails of his discovery. They were disgusted with him, felt he had given up the holy life, and soon parted company with their former friend, thinking, "The monk Gotama has become self-indulgent, he has given up the struggle and reverted to luxury."[17]

As the reactions of his five disciples demonstrate, this revelation of the Buddha's was a radical one. It smacked of self-absorption, of luxury, of reveling in emotional experience that was dangerously self-indulgent. He might as well have said he was going into therapy to nurture his inner child.

But the Buddha was indicating something very profound. Enlightenment requires the recovery of going on being.

THE KEY TO ENLIGHTENMENT

The road to enlightenment lay in this direction, the Buddha discovered, not in self-abnegation. Rather than existing in a state of reactivity, fighting against reality or clinging to it as it inexorably changes, the Buddha discovered that relaxing into his own being permitted him to relate to the world with an openness and acceptance that had been missing. While it was threatening to his followers, his path to awakening meant deepening internal experience; it meant developing more of an *inside*, through thinking, exploring, happiness, and pleasure born of seclusion. It meant building upon a capacity for joyful experience that was inherent to who he already was. This is what marked the Buddha as a great psychologist. He was not afraid to go in a more individual direction, although it was counter to the prevailing wisdom of the time.[18]

This was the seed of what became known as the Buddha's Middle Path, and he taught it with great distinction and consistency for the rest of his life. The Buddha came to see that his childhood pleasure under the rose-apple tree was the key to his enlightenment. That there could be a happiness unrelated to sensory pleasure at first glance appeared to be impossible, but it is, in fact, a reality that even Freud, whose focus was sensory pleasure, was forced to admit. While sensory pleasures derive from pursuit of pleasant physical sensations, from the instincts or erotic drives that Freud demonstrated exist even in children, there is another kind of happiness that derives from being in the moment, the joy of aliveness or at-one-ness or concentration.

Freud found evidence of this most clearly in the happiness of love, but he described it, at its most primitive and pathological, as an expression of infantile narcissism. He noted, correctly, that a child who could be happily self-involved could later develop the ability to invest that same kind of interest and attention in another person. He clearly differentiated what he called *ego libido* (or narcissism) from sexual libido, but his writings on love exhibit the same kind of reticence that his writings on mysticism reveal.

Freud was more comfortable in the terrain of common unhappiness than he was with joy, and this is a predilection that has been handed down through generations of Western psychologists.

The Buddha proclaimed the Middle Path as a means of reclaiming happiness. Both self-indulgence and self-denial were oriented around sensory pleasures, he realized. In either case, the focus was wrong. By not grasping after pleasant experiences, but by not pushing them away either, the Buddha was able to reorient himself. He was able to make use of the spontaneous being-in-the-moment of his childhood, which was not, in itself, the same as enlightenment, but which was the key to its attainment.

The Buddha's admission of fear at the time of his memory is very interesting. It is not just the Buddha who is afraid of this pleasure. Many of us take our early intimations of Buddha nature, our spontaneous expressions of love, imagination, and joy, and contaminate them with self-hatred when things go wrong in childhood. We drive them into exile for reasons that are unique to each of us. Feeling unrecognized or undeserving, we relegate that spontaneous expression to some hidden or forbidden fortress that is then lost, even to ourselves.

In the history of psychoanalysis, much has been made of the progression beyond Freud's original "drive model" of the neuroses. Freud's theory was based at first around the pleasure principle. Driven by the need for "discharge," the instincts of sex and aggression were presented as the primary modes of maximizing pleasure. Later generations of analysts recognized that people are not merely instinct-driven, but they are also person-driven. Babies are not just seeking discharge, these psychologists reasoned; they are also seeking personal contact, love, and holding. Freud neglected the eyes and the smile in his focus on the genitals, just as he neglected relationships in his focus on the personal unconscious. This latter kind of pleasure, the pleasure of interpersonal contact, has come to dominate psychological thought in the post-Freudian age. But what I recovered in meditation was something that seemed different from even the pleasures of intimacy. It was the pleasure of being, rather than of doing or being done to. While it may be a precondition for relationship, it emerged out of my own individual meditation practice. It forever counters the tendency to seek freedom from somewhere outside of myself, from a lover or a teacher or a therapist or a religion. This is not to suggest that I did not need each and every one of those relationships, for of course I did. But it was meditation that gave me a way of being that allowed me to seek them out.

The path to enlightenment requires us to recover the capacity for joy, not by imitating the Buddha's process but by initiating our own. As the Buddha found in his recovery of his childhood experience, discomfort with innate joy is understandable. Its recovery challenges basic assumptions about the origin of happiness. We are trained to assume that sensual gratification, or its absence, is the defining element of our pleasure. The Buddha found otherwise. This is part of what is revolutionary about his approach: It marks the introduction of a positive psychology to the West, one that is rooted in a radical rethinking of the route to well-being.

CHAPTER 6

PSYCHOLOGICAL EMPTINESS

The Buddha's teachings about the route to happiness were very kind to someone in my position. "It doesn't matter how well you know yourself," he seemed to say. "What matters is how you relate to what you do know." The Buddha's psychology hinged on the human capacity for self-reflection, on our peculiar ability to observe and question ourselves even as we are in the midst of a strong reaction. Whether we feel like somebody or nobody, the key is not to cling. Like Winnicott, the Buddha was always trying to show the limits of self-certainty, and he once even gave a teaching in which he explicitly refused to communicate most of what he knew. Talking one day in the forest environment that he favored, he suddenly held up a handful of *simsapa* leaves and asked the attentive bhikkhus (or monks) to tell him which was greater, the leaves in his hand or the leaves in the surrounding grove. While I have no idea what a *simsapa* leaf looks like, I have no trouble envisioning the scene. I know that I would be suspicious right away, suspecting a trick, as I am when I read over my daughter's math problems looking for how her teacher is trying to fool her.

"Very few in your hand, Lord. Many more in the grove," they replied with unsparing simplicity and none of my taste for duplicity.

It was the same with his psychological and spiritual knowledge, responded the Buddha. Like the many leaves of the *simsapa* grove, his knowledge far exceeded the handful of his teachings. Out of the vastness of all possible understanding, he taught only that which in his view led to freedom. When asked why he would not reveal other facts about reality, he gave the following reply:

"Because, friends, there is no profit in them; because they are not help-ful to holiness; because they do not lead from disgust to cessation and peace; because they do not lead from knowledge to wisdom and nirvana. That is why I have not revealed them."

The Buddha's teachings were always direct and to the point. In coming up against the world of psychotherapy, I have tried to use his words from the *simsapa* grove as a guide. "How much of this analytic wisdom is actually helpful?" I have wondered. "Does it lead to wisdom, cessation, and peace?" In the Buddhist view, knowledge is never envisioned as an end in itself but only as a beginning, useful as a means of getting oriented. As the Tibetan lama Kalu Rinpoche once put it, "It is said that someone who tries to med-itate without a conceptual understanding of what he or she is doing is like a blind person trying to find their way in open country: such a person can only wander about, with no idea how to choose one direction over another."[19] Self-knowledge must be focused if it is to be useful, thought the Buddha, and it must be focused in a specific way.

The challenge in being a psychotherapist was to find a way to stay attuned to the handful of leaves that the Buddha plucked from the *simsapa* grove while still meeting the needs of my patients. Therapy was capable of generating all kinds of insights, but they were not necessarily heading toward cessation or peace. I knew too many well-analyzed people who were just as selfish or discontent after analysis as before. They had exam-ined their lives but were not living them any differently.

MIND'S DUAL POTENTIAL

As the founder of psychoanalysis, Sigmund Freud understood how the mind can both get in its own way and seek its own freedom. In this view he was very much in accordance with his Buddhist predecessors. Always respect-ful of mind's dual capacity, Freud devised a number of strategies to elude the defensive and fearful ego, to trick the rational mind into relaxing its grip, attached as it can be to the status quo. Moving back and forth between hypnosis, dream analysis, free association, and transference, Freud was always searching to perfect his royal road to the unconscious and to open up the deeper layers of the mind. To me it seems as if Freud were always unconsciously searching for meditation.

Freud's favorite metaphor for psychoanalysis was of an archaeological dig. Not only did he prefer the archaeological metaphor, he collected archaeological antiquities. His consulting room was full of them. They represented the power of the unconscious, the mysterious forces that seep up from the depths to influence our thoughts, dreams, feelings, and behavior. They were the instincts that European civilization repressed. Freud courted these forces while at the same time remaining wary of them. He believed in radical honesty but rarely romanticized what he found.

The self extends infinitely downward, or inward, he seemed to feel. The more we can pick through the obscurations of time and decay, the more clues we can find to the earlier civilizations upon which we rest. We live primarily on the surface of things, expending a good deal of psychic energy fending off the calls of the wild. But, as Freud discovered, lives can be enriched by a relaxation of these boundaries. The unconscious might be scary, but it is also tremendously fertile. As Plato famously declared, in a phrase much celebrated within psychoanalysis, an unexamined life is not worth living.

Freud was a great explorer, and like the Greek and Roman heroes whom he so admired, his discoveries were often problematic. He positioned the ego between a hostile outer world and a volcanic inner one. He tended to find knots, complexes, and stasis; unresolvable guilt feelings; and opposing forces exhausting themselves into paralysis. Sisyphus pushing his rock, Oedipus gouging out his eyes, or Ulysses tied to his ship's mast to avoid the Sirens' call are the kinds of characters to whom Freud could relate. Blind prophets, jealous suitors, and grown men struggling to return to the breast fill his works. He created his own mythology populated by wolf men, rat men, sadistic Prussian counts, and hysterical femme fatales. He loved offending Victorian sensibilities and felt that the best protection against tyrannical forces lay in the exposure of those urges in even the most civilized men and women.

But Freud gave ample evidence of sometimes feeling stuck. He dug down to the depths but then seemed transfixed by the objects he encountered along the way. He agonized over the unpredictability of his own death, convinced that he would die in middle age. Competitively driven, his power struggles with his followers were legendary. And his method of investigation, once so full of promise, seems by the end of his life to have disappointed him. Analysis, his agent of change, started to seem, by the time of his death, interminable.

There is a story in C. S. Lewis's *Chronicles of Narnia* about a magical place between worlds, a kind of limbo zone, or way station, that permits access to a multitude of realms. This world of the "between" is filled with any number of pools of water. Some are large, some small; most seem, in my memory, to be vaguely dark and foreboding. In order to continue their journey, the adventurous children who find their way to this world have to jump into one of the pools without knowing where they will lead.

It seems to me that Freud discovered a route to this in-between place, but that once there he remained stuck. Dreams, jokes, free association, and transference all opened up cracks between worlds. They all led to that "between" that Freud named the unconscious. Yet Freud spent most of his time immersed in phenomena, swimming in the pool of infantile sexuality. The erotic underpinnings of the psyche so captivated him that he had trouble seeing past them.

Freud rescued sexuality from the repression of the Victorian era and understood its relation to what he once called the divine spark, but he hesitated to go beyond it. He opened up an important principle, that lower and higher make each other possible, but he opted for the compromise of the ego, rather than addressing the problems of the self. By the end of his life, he was ominously touting a "death drive" that he named for the Buddhist nirvana, a drive to destruction that balanced and contained his *eros*. He seemed to recognize the limitations of an exclusive focus on sexuality, but he opted for disintegration, not spirit, as the missing piece. His choice of "nirvana" as the key word is interesting. Freud would be the first to admit that there are no accidents when it comes to linguistic associations. Did he recognize, on some level, that the Buddha's theory balanced his own? Did his instincts need nirvana as a conceptual complement? The Buddha seems to be calling from another place, one that Freud heard discussed but did not completely understand, as his own equation of nirvana with death would seem to indicate.

Nirvana is the Buddha's word for freedom, not for death. It is his answer to the problem of common unhappiness, to the anxiety that is encapsulated most clearly in the fear of death. Nirvana, as the late San Francisco Zen master Suzuki Roshi put it, is the capacity to maintain one's composure in the face of ceaseless change. The key, from the Buddha's perspective, is to find nirvana through overcoming one's own self-created obstacles to that composure. The path to nirvana means working with one's own reactions to the change that surrounds us, to the change that we are. This is not a possibility that Freud ever entertained, although his method of cracking the world of appearances has important similarities to the Buddha's approach.

PSYCHOLOGICAL EMPTINESS

In the Buddhist view the major obscurations to freedom are called *kleshas*. A difficult word to translate, *kleshas* have been called everything from passions to afflictions to conflicting emotions to disturbing conceptions. No one has been able to find quite the right word, for they are not solely emotion nor are they exclusively thought. Joseph Goldstein refers to them as afflictive emotions, while the British writer and translator Stephen Batchelor has taken to calling them compulsions. The basic idea is that certain powerful reactions have the capacity to take hold of us and drive our behavior. We believe in these reactions more than we believe in anything else, and they become the means by which we both hide from ourselves and attempt to cope with a world of ceaseless change and unpredictability. The three poisons of greed, hatred, and ignorance are the classic Buddhist examples, but others include conceit, skeptical doubt, and so-called "speculative" views, notions of self that bind and restrict us.

The kleshas work by grabbing hold of consciousness and taking it over. When enraged, I do not stop to question my reality; I am completely caught up in anger. There is no space in my mind; I am identified one hundred percent with my feelings. The reason that *klesha* is so difficult to translate is that it connotes something that underlies both state of mind and emotion.

Simultaneously thought and feeling, but more basic than either, kleshas are so intense that they propel us mindlessly into actions that cause suffering. When angry, I am gripped by my anger, and I don't care, for the moment, what the consequences of my words or actions will be. I feel totally justified. Just as the ancient languages of the Buddha have only one word for head and heart, so they also recognize the power of these primitive states to monopolize the mind, body, and behavior.

When Freud talked of instincts or drives he was trying to explain a similar concept, that there are energies that permeate us, which can grab our entire being and shape who we become. But in Buddhism these energies are not seen as essential, the way they are in conventional psychoanalysis; they are seen as self-created, springing from a fundamental fear or confusion, a reaction to things being out of our control. The great eighth-century Indian Buddhist scholar Shantideva compared the kleshas to bands of thieves lying in wait to steal the jewels inside the house of mind.[20] His comparison is apt but suffers a little from self-estrangement. The bands of thieves are not separate from us. We steal from ourselves, having somehow learned how to rain on our own parades, and we are not passive victims in the matter. The trick, in Buddhist practice, is to uproot the kleshas through the insidious and invisible power of awareness. To become alert to how we restrict ourselves is to begin the process of liberation.

In Winnicott's theory, I found an explanation for the obstacle that most bedeviled me—psychological emptiness. A puzzling phenomenon that also affected a number of the people I knew, and many of those whom I treated, this emptiness was not the Buddhist kind but something more sinister. Vague feelings of being not quite real enough, of falseness or unworthiness, coupled with a sense of yearning had made me uncomfortable for a long time. Through different methods, meditation and psychotherapy had peeled much of this away for me, but I could see, through my work as a therapist and from my conversations with my peers, that the problem was a common one. Psychological emptiness seemed to me to be a particularly virulent klesha, one that defines our time and place. Winnicott was the first person I found who addressed it comprehensively. He seemed to be pulling leaves from the same *simsapa* tree as the Buddha.

To me, Winnicott's descriptions of "good enough" parenting and nonintrusive therapy were powerful evocations of what I had learned, in different language, from my meditation teachers. A child who can be lost in play with the knowledge that her parent is present but not interfering is a child who permits her ego to dissolve at the moment of good contact. This dissolution of ego is both satisfying and enriching. It feeds a sense of continuity and trust that is implicit in Winnicott's notion of what it takes to feel real. A child without enough of that experience has gaps in her capacity to go on being, with an artificially rigid ego to show for it. Meditation and psychotherapy create special circumstances in which what was once hidden away, the child's capacity for authentic experience, can begin to emerge. It is indeed possible to create a context in which a reactive self can become a responsive one. There is an experience of being that comes naturally when the mind's patterns of reactivity are quieted.

When Winnicott first wrote of going on being, in a paper published in 1949, he quoted from a patient whose depressed mother had always held her extraordinarily tightly out of fear of dropping her. This patient realized that her mother's fear had become her (the patient's) responsibility, and she assumed this burden at the expense of her own identity. This is the classic paradigm for Winnicott, and I suspect that his "patient" may well have been a stand-in for himself. The child in such a situation develops a "caretaker" self which reacts to the needs of the parent but gets in the way of self-knowledge and self-discovery, of spontaneity and daring. In this particular vignette, the mother's holding went from a reassuring embrace to an intrusion and a responsibility. The parallel to the Buddhist notion of clinging as the fundamental source of unhappiness is difficult to avoid. The mother held on out of fear and transferred that fear to her child, along with an impossible demand that her child take care of that fear for her. Instead of being free to have her own experience, the child's awareness was held hostage to her mother's need. The result was the creation of a "false self" that feels empty. It is the ultimate klesha—a compulsion, or a thief, that steals away the jewel of the mind. For Winnicott, as for the Buddha, we have to learn another way.

"At the beginning," says Winnicott's patient (sounding, as I have noted, suspiciously like Winnicott himself), "the individual is like a bubble. If the pressure from outside actively adapts to the pressure within, then the bubble is the significant thing, that is to say the infant's self. If, however, the environmental pressure is greater or less than the pressure within the bubble, then it is not the bubble that is important but the environment. The bubble adapts to the outside pressure."[21] The mother's devotion is what allows her to adapt to her baby, so that the baby does not have to adapt too much to the mother. Therapy, in Winnicott's view, is a way of equalizing this pressure, of allowing people who had been too impinged upon, or too ignored, to breathe a little more air into their bubbles.

Meditation, too, is a means of equalizing pressure. The training of awareness is also a retraining of the ego. Instead of reacting, as it was taught to do in response to the needs of the parents, the ego can learn to relax. Rather than dwelling on the past or fending off the future, the ego can melt into the present. Both meditation and psychotherapy made me feel more alive by eroding the influence of my caretaker self. Instead of always reading the environment for signs of how I was supposed to be, I began to be myself. My psychological emptiness began to fade as I came to inhabit myself more fully. In coming to dwell in my own awareness, I became less fixated on my own unworthiness. In the midst of ceaseless change, I learned how to simply go on being.

CHAPTER 7

THE KLESHA OF "I AM NOT"

This shift from unworthiness to going on being was one of the most important adjustments I could have made. As the Buddha taught, feelings of nothingness are just as destructive as those of self-centered pride. The need to see myself as having intrinsic or absolute reality could make me think I was the center of the universe or that I did not matter at all. Both were deeply engrained but limiting habits. Yet the more I was able to uncover how I was affected by this need to define myself, the more I began to open up.

This fundamental strategy of Buddhism is not something that is easily understood. I remember one early conference on Buddhism and psychotherapy in the latter part of the 1980s that a friend of mine, a psychologist named Mark Finn, organized. Buddhist masters and accomplished therapists shared their thoughts on the relevance of the two disciplines for each other. The difficulties that each side had in understanding the goals of the other became apparent very quickly. After several long presentations from the Buddhist side on the nature of emptiness and the causes of clinging, a disgruntled participant rose from the audience. "I don't care how many Zen masters can fit on the head of a pin," she began. "I want to know about shitting and pissing and fucking." There were murmurs in the crowd. Some people found her comments in bad taste, but many others essentially agreed with her. How relevant was Buddhist thought to our daily lives, to our everyday problems? Let's talk about things the way they really are! Let's get back down to basics, to the instincts and drives of Freudian theory that we all share.

One of the Tibetan lamas at the podium asked for a translation, and Mark relayed the comments through an interpreter. "She wants to know about shitting and pissing and fucking," he said, trusting that the lama would appreciate the true Zen wisdom of her comment. When hungry eat and when thirsty drink, as it were.

The lama seemed momentarily taken aback but then replied without further hesitation, "But how has she managed up until this point?"[22]

In the Buddhist view, freedom does not mean a return to a childlike simplicity, nor does it mean becoming uninhibited or spontaneous, the way we sometimes romanticize it. Freedom comes when the mind can recognize its own nature, beyond clinging, infusing the everyday with wisdom. The questioner in the audience wanted to go backward, toward an imaginary freedom that she positioned in the raw material of earthy bodily functions. Other people imagine freedom to be in some kind of transcendental realm, apart from the here-and-now of the everyday world, removed from the body and its urges.

But the Buddhist notion of freedom is different from both of these views. Recognizing that we are often estranged from our experience and detached from the moment-to-moment reality of the here-and-now, the Buddha suggested a way to cure ourselves. This did not involve exploration of the sexual and aggressive instincts per se, as Freud suggested, but instead involved the uncovering of the instinct for self-certainty.

WORKING WITH "I AM NOT"

In the ancient Buddhist literature there is a story about a conversation between a monk named Khemaka and a group of bhikkhus who quizzed him about his attainments. "Do you see within the Five Aggregates any self or anything that pertains to a self?" they asked him, referring to the five "heaps" of matter, feeling, perception, mental formations, and consciousness that traditionally are seen as the vehicles of identity. Khemaka answered that he did not. "Then why are you not fully enlightened?" they asked him, attempting to catch him in the Buddhist equivalent of false modesty.

"Because I have a feeling 'I am,' " said Khemaka, "but I do not see clearly 'This is I am.' " He knew that his feeling could not be defined precisely by classical Buddhist psychology, and yet he was aware of its influence. "It is like the smell of a flower," he continued, that is not the smell of the petals, the pollen, or the color, but of the flower, itself.[23] Even in early stages of realization, Khemaka explained, this vague sense of "I am" persists. Perhaps it is like the smell of freshly washed clothes, he suggested, and it will fade with time.

Unlike Khemaka, many of us suffer from a different kind of feeling, one that is more pernicious than that of "I am." This is the feeling of "I am not," which is extraordinarily prevalent in our time and place. The Buddha referred to this feeling in his descriptions of yearning for nonbeing, and psychoanalysis has been able to use a model of early childhood experience to explain its etiology. As theoretical as this model may seem, its implications for therapy and relevance for meditation are straightforward. When awareness is hijacked early in life by the need to react to or manage environmental insufficiencies, this hijacking leaves holes in a person's sense of self.

In talking about the annihilation that comes when going on being is interrupted, Winnicott evoked the sense of disconnection that often plagues people in the modern world. His model always focused on the need for "good-enough mothering," but it is not too much of a stretch to expand his vision to a broader cultural critique. The intense pressure in our culture for *individual* attainment affects parents and children alike. All too often, at least in situations where children are not simply being ignored, from very early in life everyone worries about what will become of a child, about who (or what) he or she is going to be. There is little trust in the natural unfolding of the individual. The pressure is there from the beginning and is transmitted at all the landmarks of development, with parents who are insecure about their own achievements conditioning their children's approach to life. Sitting up, standing, going to the bathroom, walking, and talking (events that happen, miraculously, virtually on their own) become benchmarks of progress, ways of showing off, or means of assuaging parental anxiety. The result is often a sense of personal insecurity, for if we are only performers it is difficult to feel real.

Winnicott had different ways of describing this feeling of insecurity, but he always traced it to the same hypothetical failures. At one time he described it as a residual sense of absence, as the psychological remnant of nothing happening when something might have. At another point he wrote of a "fear of breakdown" that was actually an unmetabolized memory of trauma that occurred long ago but is still feared because it was never properly worked through. And at other times he evoked a feeling of being "infinitely dropped," which he attributed to failures in the "holding environment," analogous to the bubble imagery of his early case study, in which a child's being is not supported in its own right. In each of these scenarios Winnicott described how a child's reactivity eats up, or monopolizes, awareness, making it less available for the here-and-now. Therapy, said Winnicott, is a way of giving a person a new experience in a specialized setting, of letting her accommodate to the strong emotions that were too dangerous to feel in childhood, of relaxing the inhibitions that have structured the personality.

EMOTIONAL EXPERIENCES IN MEDITATION

For many of my contemporaries, especially those without a lot of experience in psychotherapy, meditation could unexpectedly trigger intense and unusual emotional experiences. In the traditional schema of Buddhism it is recognized that strong emotions like anger, greed, worry, and agitation can disturb early efforts at concentration, but these experiences were much more frightening and strange. They could be difficult to describe yet they seemed evocative of the kind of emptiness that Winnicott knew so intimately. It was as if people fell into the gaps of their going on being under the spell of meditation and found themselves immersed, on a visceral level, in the feelings that Winnicott associated with early trauma. They seemed to recover preverbal memories, memories that could not be "known" or "understood" because they dated from a time before the onset of the conceptual or linguistic maturity that makes intellectual processing possible. These were memories that could only be felt.

It is unnerving enough to have these kinds of experiences in therapy, but to have them come up in the context of a silent meditation retreat proved challenging for many people. It was difficult to work with such feelings in the classic manner of dispassionate self-observation because of their intensity, yet in order to progress on the path of meditation it was clear that they needed to be dealt with. But how? Khemaka saw rightly that his own enlightenment depended on his ability to see "This is I am" clearly and distinctly. Yet this situation was somewhat different. We needed to do something even more difficult, to allow the feeling of "I am not" and to see it clearly and distinctly.

There are several interesting things about this feeling of "I am not." According to the Buddha, it is actually an insidious variation on "I am," and a more intransigent one to work with. There is clinging involved, and a sense of identity, but it is centered on nothingness instead of on something. There are any number of insights into this particular phenomenon in the Buddhist literature, one of most famous being that of the third-century Buddhist philosopher Nagarjuna, who remarked about the Buddhist insight into the emptiness of self, "Emptiness has been said . . . to be the relinquishment of views, but . . . those who hold to the view of emptiness are incurable."[24] Incurable is a strong word, especially for something that is turning out to be, two thousand years later, so prevalent. But Nagarjuna's warning is worth attending to. The feeling of "I am not" cannot even be compared to the smell of a flower. There is nothing so positive about it. As Winnicott noted, it's more like the feeling of being infinitely dropped.

MOVING TOWARD WHOLENESS

Much of my work in psychotherapy consists in working with this feeling of "I am not" in one form or another. It is a major psychological block to spiritual attainment. I was lucky enough to confront my own version of this problem through both meditation and therapy. Each one seemed to empower the other. Meditation showed me that awareness has a place of primacy versus the ego and whatever sense of unworthiness might fill my consciousness. But psychotherapy helped me to see how I perpetuated my own sense of isolation by restricting that very awareness. It showed me how I was afraid of other people and what could be done to change that. It did this by engaging me in a relationship that eased me through my fears and blind spots.

Working with personal emptiness required a kind of interpersonal meditation, where the therapist's own attentional skills were brought to bear on my self's "bubble."

In much the same way that my therapist challenged my use of the phrase "parts of me" or demanded that I speak directly to him, he would also ask me to rephrase my words whenever I spoke in the passive voice.

"Anger is coming up in me," I would sometimes say, conditioned as I was by meditation to objectify my inner experience. "Say that again but start your sentence with 'I,'" Isadore would reply, forcing me to speak from the inside, instead of looking in on myself from the periphery. For a long time I wondered if this was in some way anti-Buddhist. "Why should I start my sentences with 'I' if the I does not exist?" I would wonder, but I think such questioning was more a sign of my clinging to emptiness than a true reading of Buddhism. Speaking from the inside required me to be at one with my experience, instead of operating at a protective distance. It forced me to experience myself more directly, to improvise, and to take chances in my expression of myself.

I was eager for this shift but also hesitant, unsure what I would talk about in therapy and secretly afraid that I could not come up with anything interesting enough. I always hoped to remember a dream from the night before so that I would have something to begin my session with, and I would rehearse what I was going to say, as I used to do in high school before going on my first dates. The feeling of discomfort when I ran out of material was excruciating. There was something about dropping into those moments of intense anxiety that felt utterly familiar and completely dreadful, like being caught in a whirlpool or spun down a drain. Yet out of those situations would often come moments of true relating that soothed and relieved me. I could feel myself exhale.

Through such experiences things began to make sense to me. Psychological emptiness masks an agony, or a conglomeration of agonies, that are too difficult to bear at the time of their genesis. These agonies live inside of us but outside of our awareness, as if waiting for the opportunity to be known.[25] Knowing them means experiencing them in all of their horror, but this can only be done in a particular context, one that is safe enough to hold them. The isolation of a meditation retreat is not always most conducive to the processing of such material.

People come to therapy plagued with a sense of personal unworthiness but propelled by a movement toward wholeness. They reproduce, in their relationship with the therapist, all of their reactive coping mechanisms, all of the ways in which they successfully manage to avoid their own particular agonies, and yet, if the therapy is done skillfully, they start to process the feelings they have never allowed themselves to know. A patient of mine says to me out of the blue, "You must think I'm the most boring person in the world." Another woman tells me, startled and embarrassed, that she has the feeling that I want to slap her across the face because she is so annoying. These are momentary realities for my patients, and I know I am not feeling anything of the sort. To me, these sudden confessions are signs of the klesha "I am not," but (as Khemaka would say) they do not see clearly this "I am not." If therapy is to be useful, these patients will begin to see it all too clearly. The agony of being held too tightly, of being left too alone, or of feeling somehow wrong can start to be digested. As these feelings are owned, the gaps in going on being are metabolized. The person can emerge. The reactive, caretaker self that papers over the empty, unworthy one loses its primacy of place. Something new can start to happen. Going on being dusts itself off, and awareness starts to find itself.

THE VALUE OF THERAPY

When the klesha of "I am not" is particularly tenacious, a personal relationship seems to be most effective in getting back on track. In spiritual communities this function may be served by the senior teachers or by the group, but in our secular society there is often no one to assume this role— no one but a therapist, that is. The Buddha was able to leapfrog this stage by remembering back to his joy under the rose-apple tree while watching his father work, but many of us do not have his ability for self-analysis.

When the capacity for awareness has been hijacked, a therapeutic relationship is often an important intermediate step. Looking may be the key, as the Sufi Nasruddin taught, but sometimes we need to be seen as well.

A recent interaction with a patient reinforced this for me. Jan is a writer, but one who consistently destroyed what she wrote. Either she threw it away before anyone else could see it, or she erased it through endless and perfectionistic rewriting in an effort to (supposedly) improve it. The night before our session she had a dream, in which a man from work whom she admired offered her a lot of cash for her essays. I felt immediately that, in some ways, I was that man. I was always encouraging her efforts, despite her protestations. She took the cash but then proceeded to shit all over it, feeling a familiar sense of humiliation and shame as she sat in a pile of cast-off newspapers surrounded by the soiled money.

As we talked about the dream, several things became clear. The dream mirrored Jan's creative process. She would often begin with a burst of inspiration, but her reworking would render her words lifeless and dull. It was as if she were coloring them over with darker and darker hues, the way she smeared feces on the money in her dream. But there was another element to the mirroring as well. In her writing, Jan reproduced a process that had happened in her life—any kind of bold, bright declaration of her own energy had to be turned into humiliation, just as any interest from another person had to be denigrated. She was replicating in her behavior something that she had already experienced but had not completely dealt with— the shaming of her own self-expression by her creative, competitive, and insecure parents. Compulsively destroying any vestige of spontaneity in her work, she did not believe that she was capable of making anything worthwhile.

This dream emerged after years of therapy, in the context of a therapeutic relationship that had already developed its own history. I had no way of knowing if it would prove transformative or if the dream and the subsequent realizations would fade away and be forgotten. But I believed that the potential was there for Jan to both know her shame and to come through it. Her most secret identifications were being brought into awareness through the vehicle of our relationship. She had the opportunity to know them as nothing but thoughts and feelings, as that curious conglomeration of mind and body that Buddhists call kleshas. Bringing them forward through her dream and privileging me with their content gave her the chance to complete something. She was humiliated by her young and inexperienced parents—it was not an illusion—and this had scarred her perception of herself. She had the chance now to do something different instead of simply acting it out in semidisguised form. Going on being might yet come to the fore.

Some weeks later Jan came to see me with another dream. She did not tell me about it until well into the session, but we still had time to talk about some of its implications. She was in a huge and cavernous hall, something like a cross between the Metropolitan Museum of Art and Grand Central Station, and she was clutching an important valise that contained all of her important papers, her writing as well as the deed to her house. Suddenly, the valise was lost and she was in a panic, looking everywhere for it. Her friend was by her side, a vain and superficial woman who kept telling her to forget about it, to come join her at a party she was going to. Jan did not want to go to the party; she needed to find her valise. The scene shifted to the basement of the museum, an endless corridor filled with lockers. Jan reached for a flashlight to look for her papers, and she woke up as she was on her hands and knees in the dirt searching for them.

Jan's associations came fast and furious. "That's what I have to do in my writing," she said first, as she talked about what it was like on her hands and knees peering under the basement lockers of the Metropolitan Museum of Art. "Looking in the dirt—I was happy doing that, like a pig in shit." I told her the story of Nasruddin, looking under the lamppost for his keys. Therapy was opening up the process of looking: searching for her voice, or, as Winnicott would have it, for her true self. Her friend was calling to her to forget about it, to come to the party and put on her false front, but Jan would have none of it. She wanted the flashlight, and she wanted to look around.

Then Jan remembered her first confession. The priest asked her if she had sinned, and she cast about for something to tell him. As she recalled, "I was seven or eight, what could I have done that was so bad?" But she remembered one thing to tell the waiting priest. Some days before, she was on her hands and knees looking under the radiators in her house, just as she was in the dream. She found a penny glistening there in the dust and wondered whether to tell her mother about it or keep it for herself. The decision to keep the penny became her first sin. Even then, her obligation to her priest/mother overshadowed the pleasure of discovery. The brightness of the penny, like the cash in her first dream, was soiled.

Jan's dreams and her subsequent memory beautifully illustrate Winnicott's concept of going on being. As the psychoanalyst Michael Eigen has written, "The spontaneous sense of going on being provides the home-base feeling of self, a basis of normal feeling and feeling normal. . . ."[26] Jan did not feel normal, as a person or as a writer. That is why she sought therapy. From as far back as the incident with the penny, her joy of spontaneous discovery was contaminated. Like the valise of her dream, this nugget of self-confidence was lost to her. When it leaked out into her writing, she felt compelled to destroy it, repeating over and over again the pattern that had conditioned her mind. But through the therapy relationship Jan began to reawaken. She made contact with her inherent sense of all-rightness, what Michael Eigen calls normality or aliveness and which Winnicott called going on being. Her exclusive identification with "I am not" was challenged, and she could proceed.

PART FOUR

At first one develops understanding by relying on training. Later, one develops realization by summoning forth personal experience in one's mindstream through examination and analysis. But the situation is such that mere understanding and realization will not bring freedom; even though one has food, for example, one will not be satisfied if one does not eat it.

—Dudjom Lingpa, *Buddhahood without Meditation:
A Visionary Account Known as Refining Apparent Phenomena*

CHAPTER 8

THE PROBLEM OF THE EMOTIONS

When I began to practice meditation, a curious thing happened. I thought I was watching my breath, but I was parenthetically learning to watch my mind. My teachers told me to "note" my thoughts when my attention wandered, but they did not let on to how relentless this process could be. My thoughts were much more plentiful than my breath was. "Thinking, thinking," I would say to myself as I caught myself in the act of a thought. It would abate for a moment, and I would struggle to locate my breathing, but two seconds later I would be thinking again. I was amazed at how tenacious my thoughts could be and how little they had to offer. Very rarely would I have a new thought; mostly I simply repeated the old ones over and over again.

I could see two distinct patterns to my thinking, how I oscillated between two overriding modes. In one, I was the critical but somewhat distant observer, judging myself and the faults of those around me. In the other, I would feel sorry for myself for a variety of reasons that centered on how alone I could feel. I could go back and forth between these two poles, but I was rarely free of one or the other. I began to think of myself as a character in an old Batman movie, stuck inside a room whose walls are slowly compressing, trying with all my might to hold them apart with my arms and legs. It was very narrow in there. The great bulk of my mental energy was taken up with one or both of these patterns, and I could feel myself squeezed between them.

In learning how to watch my breath, I was also being introduced to my mind. There was no avoiding it. I was startled to discover how critical I could be, how a thin layer of judgment entered into my relationships with other people and even into my relationship with myself. This criticalness sometimes took the form of seeing other people's faults and feeling superior or seeing my own faults and feeling dissatisfied. In either case, this judgmental posture reinforced the distance and aloofness that made me feel unhappy. I knew myself via my judgments, but I was also short-circuiting my experience by assuming that they were the last word on everything. And then I was cutting myself off even more in self-pity.

AWAKENING

As I came to see how dominated I was by such patterns, I worked very carefully to begin to release myself from them. I could think such things, I realized, but I did not have to believe them. Just because I thought them did not mean I had to always follow their lead. When the critical thoughts would come, I could simply notice them, sometimes commenting, "judging, judging" to myself. When I would begin to feel sorry for myself, I could note that also, and I would then try to bring myself back to my immediate experience rather than going off into an all-too-familiar and habitual train of thought.

As I look back, I can see that this was the beginning of an important shift. Something new was beginning to happen. In the place of unrestrained judgment or reflexive self-pity I began to notice a complex array of feelings. It was as if all the critical commentary was obscuring a range of emotion that had been previously out of reach. Beneath my judgments lay a kind of apprehension or fear, while behind my self-pity was a feeling of apology. While neither of these were particularly pleasant, experiencing them felt better than avoiding them. They did not necessarily last as long as I would have thought, and they often gave way in unexpected directions. Fear could sometimes become excitement, for instance, as I allowed myself to engage more openly. Self-pity, and the apology behind it, sometimes dissolved spontaneously, as I became less critical of the feelings I seemed to be carrying.

My internal experience became deeper, richer, and more complicated. I felt myself coming alive. In psychodynamic language, I would say that my authentic self, in the form of emotional experience, began to open up to my awareness. I had been secretly afraid of how desolate my internal landscape had felt, but now I was confronted with the reality of my living, breathing, and emotional body. I felt a vitality in my newfound emotional responsiveness that gave me some feeling for what the Buddha meant when he described himself as "awake." At the time I was confused by all of this, even though in my heart I knew it was right. Was this just another level of distraction, part of my ongoing "melodrama," as Ram Dass would sometimes say, or was this something more essential? It certainly felt essential, but my mind was not sure. I looked to the Buddhist community for guidance, but it turned out that they were not so sure, either.

THE PROBLEM OF EMOTIONAL LIFE

Even in the Buddhist world, people seemed to be of two minds about feelings. On the one hand, nirvana was defined as the absence of greed, hatred, and ignorance, as the development of a pervasive equanimity. The emotions, in this view, seemed to be the enemy, much the way the passions were sometimes viewed in the Western religious traditions. On the other hand, the route to nirvana was clearly through the development of an accepting attitude toward all aspects of experience including emotions. This meant making room for them, even if they made me uncomfortable, developing a kind of tolerance for the most disturbing aspects of the psyche.

I soon found, though, that it was difficult to talk to some Buddhist teachers about emotional experience, since the language of many of the Eastern traditions seemed to have no words for what I was trying to express. In Tibetan, for instance, there is no way to say, "How are you?"; one can only say, "How is your body?" There is not even a word for emotion in the Tibetan language, only one for what translates as *"afflictive* emotion." This made early discussions between Buddhist teachers like the Dalai Lama and Western psychotherapists very problematic. There was no vocabulary within the Tibetan tradition for concepts like self-hatred or low self-esteem, and there was therefore no experience of dealing with them from a Buddhist perspective. There was also no way to speak of emotional experience in a completely positive way, because of the inherently negative cast that the Tibetan language imparted to the word.

In many of the Eastern traditions, of course, the word "mind" encompasses more than just the organ of thought. The mind is not even localized in the head. It extends to the heart, so that one word represents both concepts. If you were to ask a Tibetan monk to point to his mind, for example, he would most likely point to his chest rather than to his brain. The Tibetan mind flows between the heart and the crown of the head, circulating through much of the body in a series of channels, wheels, and vortexes that are detailed in esoteric medical texts. In addition, the body is experienced as much more than just raw physical sensation. It is alive to feeling, much of which seems to correspond to what we think of as emotion. But the Eastern "mind" did not seem to experience the emotional body in the same way that I instinctively did, as a kind of third force, or intermediate zone, between mind and body. This left me feeling unsure as I pursued my meditative training. How could I work with this deepening and expanding emotional body that lurked behind my thinking mind?

Just as Ram Dass taught me the basics of Right Understanding and Joseph Goldstein the essentials of Right Meditation, so did Jack Kornfield orient me to the emotions. Just back from monkhood in Thailand, Jack was teaching at Naropa as the first step in his reintegration into America when I met him. He had gone deeply into the world of solitary retreat in the forest tradition of Thailand after serving in the Peace Corps there, but for me the thrust of his teaching was always about integrating a spiritual understanding with one's life in the world. Perhaps it was because he was so familiar with renunciation that he could emphasize this integration, or perhaps it was his need to integrate the spiritual dimension that had sent him into the monasteries in the first place. I was not sure. But as I contemplated the Buddha's Eightfold Path, I could see that Jack's subtle emphasis was often on those aspects linked by our emotional lives that are grouped together as Right Relationship (Right Speech, Right Action, and Right Livelihood). This is not to suggest that Jack did not teach the full range of the Buddha's philosophy, for he was (and is) a wonderful and inspirational meditation teacher, but he was always willing to embrace the emotional and relational dimensions as indispensable to an integrated spiritual understanding.

Jack had an instinctive feel for the sense of self-estrangement that had led me to feel so distanced from myself. He liked to quote the story of a man from one of James Joyce's novels who lived his life always one step removed from his experience. Jack knew that there was a difference between what I thought I felt and what I actually felt, and he understood, from his own experience, how the power of awareness could heal this split. "The mind creates the abyss, and the heart crosses it," Jack often repeated, quoting an Indian guru known as the *bidi wallah*, a teacher who was enlightened from his perch on an Indian street-corner selling inexpensive cigarettes (or *bidis*) to passersby. I cannot imagine a more beautiful evocation of Winnicott's theory of going on being than this. Intimately familiar with this abyss when I met Jack, I was delighted to find someone who was not afraid of it.

Jack was the first teacher whom I ever approached personally. He was not necessarily the most approachable person, but I think I felt comfortable with him right off the bat, perhaps recognizing a similar background (we both had scientist fathers) or certain similarities in our personalities. He was teaching a class on insight meditation that I attended eagerly, and I seized the first opportunity to make a private appointment with him, hoping to find some guidance for my senior thesis idea about insight. Jack was not famous, but had appeared at Naropa out of nowhere, having been introduced to the Tibetan founder of Naropa, Chögyam Trungpa, some months earlier. Trungpa asked him to teach at the last minute. Perhaps this helped make him seem less intimidating to me.

A PATH WITH HEART

I remember coming to the door of Jack's townhouse apartment one afternoon and knocking and hearing no reply. I waited a moment, self-conscious, and then pushed open the unlocked door. It was very still inside, and I caught a glimpse of a solitary figure lying on a couch in the next room. As I made a bit of a disturbance, the figure raised himself slowly to standing. Jack was so thin, he reminded me of a single grain of rice, one of those seeds upon which great Japanese artists have painted the world. He was colorfully dressed, in a vest with Afghani overtones, and his face, with its pronounced, angular features and dark hair, made me think of the Turkish Empire or such entirely unfamiliar places as Uzbekistan or Samarkand. He sniffled slightly from allergies as he approached.

Jack was doing a lying-down meditation, he explained to me, as his energy began to return. The Buddha taught that meditation could be undertaken in four postures: sitting, standing, walking, and lying-down. Awareness did not have to be something special, saved for a prescribed period of the day; it could integrate and suffuse our daily lives, filling in the spaces between interactions. This was immediately interesting to me. Before I could even ask my questions, I was learning something. I was familiar with meditation that could be done once or twice a day, as a treatment for stress or high blood pressure or as a spiritual exercise, but I had not quite realized that it had the potential to enter into daily life in such a practical way. Here was someone who was consciously making this a reality.

Jack was twenty-eight years old at the time, a graduate of Dartmouth, and a veteran of the Peace Corps and several years as a Buddhist monk in Burma and Thailand. To me, he seemed incredibly accomplished, and all grown up. With a restlessness that stood out in sharp contrast to the calm he projected in my interview with him, Jack had scoured the Buddhist world of Southeast Asia collecting the oral teachings of great meditation masters. He had the manuscript of these interviews with him; they were later collected and published as his first book, *Living Buddhist Masters*. (As the years passed and I continued to study with Jack, some of us began to refer to this book as "Dead Buddhist Masters," but for the moment these teachings were very much alive under Jack's careful stewardship.) Sometime that summer, as if in answer to my pursuit of written knowledge about Buddhist insight, Jack told me the story that eventually closed the introduction to this book. One day a famous woman lecturer came to his meditation master, Ajahn Chah, to tell him about her work lecturing on the Buddhist psychology called Abhidharma in Bangkok. Her students seemed to get so much from this approach. "Do you not agree with how important it is for students to study Buddhist psychology and metaphysics?" she asked.

"Oh, yes," he replied, "very important."

Encouraged, she asked him whether he had his own students learn Abhidharma.

"Indeed," he responded.

And what books did he think were best, she wondered. Where did he recommend they begin?

"Only here," he said, pointing to his heart. "Only here."[27]

This was the message that Jack continually emphasized to me. All of my pursuit of knowledge and understanding had to be centered in my heart. This meant that my emotional life could not be pushed away or ignored. I had to learn a faith in emotional experiencing that would allow me to make use of the vitality I was uncovering. We fear our feelings precisely because they have the power to overwhelm us. Our conventional self, who we think we are, disappears in the heat of passion or excitement or sorrow. We fear this loss of self because it reminds us of what a tenuous hold we have on ourselves in the first place. In guarding against this flood of feeling, we make use of our intellects and retreat into a critical or judgmental mode. But this is unnecessary to perpetuate. The self that we are afraid of losing is a false self. If we can learn not to fear our feelings, we gain access to the real. We have the opportunity to reclaim going on being.

THE MEANING OF RESTRAINT

This is not to suggest that the Buddha did not teach restraint of the emotions, for he surely did. "Anger gallops like a wild chariot," he said in the *Dhammapada*. "Hold it firm, steady it! Be the true charioteer—don't just finger the reins."[28] But the route to this control is always through "clear seeing." To restrain the emotion, the Buddha taught, you do not have to actually restrain the emotion, you only have to restrain the reaction to the emotion that leads to impulsive action. And this cannot be done punitively. "Force is not Dhamma, who uses it, not righteous. Only he is wise who sees clearly before acting."[29] In describing Right Action, this caveat became extremely important to me. Restraining the emotions did not need to involve the use of force; I could rely on the gentle use of investigation, replacing the urgency of action with the curiosity of self-discovery.

When Jack was returning to America from his years in Thailand, he sought out an elderly Western monk and asked him if he had any advice about being back in the West. "Only one thing," said the monk. "When you're running to catch the subway and you see it leaving without you, don't panic, just remember, 'There's always another train.'" I always liked this notion, even before I moved to New York and realized how impossible it was to implement. But it took me a while to appreciate how applicable it was in emotional situations that seemed to bear no resemblance to catching a train. The monk did not suggest indifference to the subway leaving the station, but he pointed to where control is possible. "Don't panic and go running after it," he suggested. Rather than letting disappointment turn into anxiety or self-pity, learn to see the disappointment clearly while restraining the action. Stay with the original feeling longer. Cultivate patience.

The willingness to stay in the uncomfortable feeling when there is nothing else to be done is the cornerstone of Buddhist wisdom. "There's always another train," became a metaphor for me for how resistant I was to enduring frustration. As I worked to change my coping strategies, I found that I did not have to go running after every lost opportunity. In fact, I discovered an important, if latent, capacity. I could wait.

FOLLOWING THE AFFECT

There is a saying in therapy, "Follow the affect." Following the affect means not being distracted by the content of a person's story but instead attending to the emotional reality of what the person is saying and how he or she is saying it. It is one of those teachings that, with luck, you hear at the beginning of your education as a therapist, because it helps you all the way through. Meditation, for me, was training in following the affect. I learned how to do it well before anyone ever taught me the phrase. If you follow the affect in a psychotherapy session, you can untangle the person's unstated therapy needs. If you follow the affect in meditation, you can uncover some latent and more fundamental quality of openness and clarity of mind. As Winnicott described, the false self is predominantly a mental construction in which the secondary process is put to use managing a difficult environment. The hallmark of this "caretaker" self is an overly mental, super-rational approach to life. Feelings break open the contraction of this false self.

Jack's willingness to embrace the emotional body made it possible to use meditation to follow the affect back to its source. For many of us this meant using our feelings of shame, anger, unworthiness, yearning, or sadness to trace a path back to those moments in time when our natural openness, excitement, or self-expression was frustrated in one way or another. The details of the story turned out not to be as important as the discovery that our capacities for love and joy were not, in fact, lost in childhood, even if traumatic things had happened. This is what Jack's teacher Ajahn Chah was getting at when he pointed so deliberately at his heart.

In Buddhist psychology emotions are classified as "skillful" or "unskillful." The "afflictive" ones of anger, envy, pride, worry, agitation, and greed are opposed by their counterparts of love, compassion, humility, patience, tranquility, and generosity. The model is a simple one: two opposites cannot occupy the same psychic space. Anger impedes and occludes love, and vice versa. Turn one down by cultivating the other. But there is another way of understanding this model, one that is more attuned to the ambiguities of contemporary psychoanalysis. In this view, the skillful and unskillful emotions are opposite because they are part of a single dialectic. Anger is a perversion of love, transformed in the crucible of frustration. Anxiety is restricted excitement. Envy is a contracted form of empathy, since both spring from the capacity to know another's experience. Much of Tibetan Buddhism's vast iconography is actually a visual demonstration of these relationships. Wrathful deities represent the transformation of anger into the energy of "cutting through" the ego. The benevolent figure of the goddess Green Tara is green with an envy that is transmuted into empathy. Naked and lustful dancers represent the relationship of passion to joyful embrace. In Jack's book *A Path With Heart*, he gives a description of his own process in meditation that makes this kind of dynamic very clear.

In Jack's case, his struggle in meditation was with sexual fantasy. There was an insistent and compulsive quality to his fantasies that made him feel ashamed and that kept him from applying the same acceptance to his erotic yearnings that he had learned to train on his other mental and physical experiences. While his teacher counseled him to accept things just as they were, he had great resistance in this particular realm. Finally, he decided to investigate his cravings more deeply. To his surprise, he found that almost every time his fantasies were strong there was also a feeling of loneliness. The fantasies seemed to be a way of seeking comfort for himself. As ashamed as he was of the compulsive nature of his sexual ideation, he had even more aversion for his loneliness. With great effort he stayed with those feelings, only to discover what sounded like a child's voice repeating something that translated as, "There is something insufficient and wrong with me, and I will always be rejected."

Supported by the quiet and calm of his concentrated mind and by the gentle guidance of his teacher, Jack went further still. He felt deep into his body where the loneliness seemed to reside and sensed what seemed like a hole or space. This was a graphic representation of Winnicott's "gap" in going on being. Filled with yearning, hunger, and emptiness, and corroded with shame and self-pity, this space seemed to open and become clearer as Jack relaxed his judgments about it. "I let it open as much as it wanted, instead of closing around it as I had done for so many years," Jack writes. Instead of reacting with shame or aversion, he learned to leave the feelings alone. A transformation took place. Although the hole remained empty, its hungry quality diminished, and his experience was clearer and more open. Feelings of peace and contentment arose. He could see himself simultaneously in both a contracted state of loneliness and an expanded one of fulfillment, and he knew without a doubt that his fear-based self was only a fraction, or contraction, of his true nature.[30] With that experience to guide him, Jack lost his fear of the painful emotions. He knew that behind them lay the ceaseless heartbeat of going on being.

THE PURSUIT OF PLEASURE

Within Jack's story is a very important psychological lesson about the pursuit of pleasure. If he had remained preoccupied with erotic fantasy, he could never have made his breakthrough, but if he had tried to clamp down on those fantasies, he also would have remained frustrated. In either case the attachment to pleasure would have gotten the better of him. By exploring his desire instead of acting it out, he was able to discover what the yearning obscured. The Buddha made the very important point that there is another kind of happiness besides sensual gratification, one that the attachment to erotic fantasy tends to hide. This other kind of happiness, that of going on being, is a birthright that is often lost to the pursuit of pleasure.[31] We lose touch with our own intrinsic happiness as we start to search for external gratification, and we assume it is gone forever. As Jack found, his erotic fantasies were ultimately an expression of his desire to return to that fundamental joy, but they could also be the means of obstructing it.

Jack's story is an inspiring example of how the obstructions to awakening can be removed. Under the guidance of his meditation master, he had done the most difficult thing I could imagine. Following his affect, he was like an explorer tracking a river to the mountain springs that feed it. Heading upstream instead of being driven heedlessly away from his goal, all at once he was surprised at the gushing that came swelling from his heart. His transformation was both spiritual and psychological. What distinguished it, for me, was the hope that it inspired. This was not a story that ended in paralysis or compromise. There was no ironic twist that left him disappointed and alone. Change was truly possible, it seemed, through the cultivation of awareness.

When the Buddha taught meditation, he often used examples from everyday life to help his disciples understand the kind of balanced attention that he was recommending. Two of the most commonly repeated examples were those of the lute and the plow. Farming and musical instruments seem to have been common knowledge in the Buddha's day, and his words still retain some of their resonance, even for those of us who have little familiarity with either. In one case, he instructed a man named Sona, who prided himself on being the most energetic of disciples but who was still unable to find the freedom that the Buddha had promised.

"Tell me, Sona," said the Buddha, "In earlier days were you not skilled in playing string music on a lute?"

"Yes, Lord."

"And tell me, Sona, when the strings of your lute were too taut, was then your lute tuneful and easily playable?"

"Certainly not, O Lord."

"And when the strings of your lute were too loose, was then your lute tuneful and easily playable?"

"Certainly not, O Lord."

"But when, Sona, the strings of your lute were neither too taut nor too loose, but adjusted to an even pitch, did your lute then have a wonderful sound and was it easily playable?"

"Certainly, O Lord."

"Similarly, Sona, if energy is applied too strongly, it will lead to restlessness, and if energy is too lax it will lead to lassitude. Therefore, Sona, keep your energy in balance and balance the Spiritual Faculties and in this way focus your attention."[32]

In one way or another, balancing the spiritual faculties was always the thrust of the Buddha's teachings. It was another means of teaching the Middle Path, of preventing people from making the same kinds of mistakes as the Buddha made before his revelatory memory about the rose-apple tree. By faculties, according to the classical psychology, he meant something very specific. The mental factors of faith, energy, wisdom, mindfulness, and concentration, like the factors of absorption, begin as undeveloped potentials but can be cultivated to the point of strength and stability. While the development of the factors of absorption is the thrust of the beginning phase of meditation, more advanced practice consists of the subtle balancing of these five faculties, both individually, as in the case of Sona the lute player, and together. Faith and wisdom have to be balanced, as do concentration and energy. Mindfulness is said to be like the lead horse of the pack of five—if the ability to maintain moment-to-moment awareness is maintained, the others naturally follow.

LEARNING FROM CHILDREN

While the Buddha's metaphors remain helpful in giving a sense of the balance required in meditation, I have found that raising children is full of even more relevant examples. Perhaps it is my training as a psychiatrist that has steered me in this direction, or perhaps it is our twentieth-century distance from the natural world that has necessitated finding new metaphors. Certainly in the Buddha's time the emphasis was on renouncing family life, not using it as a model for meditation. But training the mind is a lot like raising a child. It requires the same ongoing attention, the same balance of care and *laissez-faire*, the same willingness to hang in there with the whole range of difficult and exhilarating phenomena.

When dealing with a child's anger, for example, Winnicott proposed that the task of the parent is simply to survive. The two extremes of retaliation or abandonment are to be avoided, since either is a threat to the child's well-being, even though one of them may be our first impulse. When my children, for example, suddenly explode with, "I hate you," because of some limit I am imposing, I have trained myself to respond calmly but firmly, "You might hate me, but you still have to do what I say." I do this despite the fact that I am horrified to hear them say that they hate me. But for them to see that I can survive their rage is more important than my personal reaction. It has helped them to know anger as something that is manageable, not an out-of-control force that can destroy that which they need and love.

This ability to simply survive, not to retaliate and not to abandon, is another definition of mindfulness. It is analogous to that other middle path that is so important in child rearing—the balance between interfering and ignoring. A parent has to continuously adjust the balance between helping children and staying out of the way, just as a meditator has to find the middle ground between straining and lassitude.

I had an unexpected experience with my eight-year-old son one summer in Maine that made me understand this in a new way. Setting out early on an impromptu canoe trip from one small Penobscot Bay island to the next, we urged him over and over again to eat a good breakfast so he would not be hungry later. As is his tendency, he refused. We went to a neighboring island where our friends were camping. They had only seven-grain bread and natural-style peanut butter to offer us for lunch, in a picnic spot that was suddenly raided by yellow jackets. My son not unexpectedly rejected this food, and on the long trip home began to whine with unmistakable hunger. We berated him with "I told you so," and then commanded him to tell us what lesson he had learned from all of this. He was hunched over on a seat in the rear of the canoe, looking a bit like a prisoner of war with a big orange life jacket hung dejectedly around his neck.

"Eat when you're not hungry," he replied, looking up at us with a defiant twinkle in his eye.

My psychotherapist mind was aghast. We all laughed, and he knew he had trumped us, but I could suddenly see the pattern we were laying down. By interfering too much in the natural process of hunger and eating, we were in danger of forging a compliant or resistant self instead of an authentic one. My son's ability to use humor to fend us off was admirable, but we were still erring on the side of interference. In Zen Buddhism they say,

"When hungry, eat; when thirsty, drink," and I have often wondered if they are being simplistic or profound. Yet as my son's experience revealed, even these most basic urges of hunger or thirst become complicated. How often do we eat or drink out of some other motivation than hunger or thirst? In learning to live (or eat) prophylactically, are we just ending up afraid? What was the better lesson for my son, to eat when he had no appetite or to learn to tolerate his hunger? What is the better lesson for us, to try to fend off the future or to meet it with arms, and stomach, open?

My continuing investigation of Buddhism has required a willingness to adjust and readjust my mental posture, just as dealing with my children has. Self-indulgence and self-denial, effort and surrender, and idealization and skepticism have all had to be given their turns. "Keep your energy in balance and balance the Spiritual Faculties," said the Buddha to Sona the musician. Faith without wisdom is only blind faith, while wisdom without faith can be righteous, or anxious. Only by returning to mindfulness is it possible to find the balance required.

UNCOVERING RAPTURE

The five spiritual faculties of faith, energy, wisdom, concentration, and mindfulness grow within the path of mindfulness but are dependent on the path of concentration and the factors of absorption that are strengthened therein. This is yet another of the delicate balancing acts that meditation requires. At the clearing of access concentration, when the first meditative stability is accomplished and the hindrances are no longer overwhelming, the meditator has a choice. Access concentration is that time in meditation when the first stability of mind is achieved, when the five hindrances are quieted such that it is possible to stay with the flow of inner experience for limited periods of time. One can proceed on the path of concentration, developing the rapture, joy, and one-pointedness of what Freud, in a correspondence with a yoga practitioner, once called the oceanic feeling. Alternatively, a meditator can choose to focus on the practice of bare attention, noting whatever is arising in the mind-body continuum in a movement toward equanimity. "Imitate the sands of the Ganges," said the ninth-century Chinese Zen teacher Huang Po of this approach, "who are not pleased by perfume and who are not disgusted by filth." The Ganges, of course, is India's holiest river, revered as a "mother," whose shores are the site of both worship and cremation. Perfume and filth do indeed reside upon the river's sands.

The big surprise to me, even though it was stressed in all the classical texts, was how indispensable feelings of joy were in establishing a foundation in mindfulness. It seemed like cheating to have a religion that stressed the inevitability of unsatisfactoriness be so strongly based in the availability of joy. Yet this became another of the paradoxes that so delighted me about Buddhism.

The link between concentration and mindfulness is the mental factor of rapture. Rather than being a kind of out-of-the-body experience, in Buddhism rapture is defined as intensified interest in the object of awareness. Instead of becoming blissed out, as I had naively imagined, a meditator who strengthens the factors of absorption develops the ability to be "blissed in." Thus, in concentration meditations, interest or fascination with the central object of meditation keeps the mind involved with it. In mindfulness, this same quality of interest keeps the mind open, engaged with shifting objects of awareness, with the same fascination that a baby exhibits with a new toy, turning it every which way. As the composer John Cage once summarized, "In Zen they say: If something is boring for two minutes, try it for four. If still boring, try it for eight, sixteen, thirty-two, and so on. Eventually one discovers that it's not boring at all but very interesting." Energy, mindfulness, concentration, and faith all depend on high degrees of rapture; it is one of the engines of meditation. For me, it was this quality more than any other that surprised and delighted me in my early retreats. I was eager to learn what the classical texts had to say, since there was very little attention paid to it in Western psychology.

Rapture was reported to be of five grades—minor, momentary, showering, uplifting, and pervading, and its function was said to be to refresh the mind. "Minor happiness is only able to raise the hairs on the body," said the *Visuddhimagga*. "Momentary happiness is like flashes of lightning at different moments. Showering happiness breaks over the body again and again like waves on the seashore. Uplifting happiness (seems) powerful enough to levitate the body and make it spring up into the air. . . . But when pervading (rapturous) happiness arises, the whole body is completely pervaded, like a filled bladder, like a rock cavern invaded by a huge inundation."[33] Rapture has the specific function of suppressing hatred, while joyful feelings inhibit worry and restlessness. It is difficult to be angry when your body is pervaded by a rapturous inundation.

Of the five spiritual faculties, the only one not directly encouraged by this quality of rapture is wisdom. It is possible, in the Buddhist view, to have much happiness but little understanding. But the reverse is also true. We can have insight without happiness. This is borne out in many long-term relationships. As couples start to notice, they can have tremendous wisdom about each other's characters but little of the idealization that once marked their love. The balance is easily lost. To reach for insight (in love, meditation, or therapy) without a corresponding ease and balance is often a recipe for anxiety, or destruction.

THE DEGRADATION OF ROMANCE

As a therapist, I have counseled many refugees from meditation retreats who have become frightened by how alone they could feel in the silence of the meditation hall, just as I have seen many individuals who have lost their faith in love under the pressures of a long-term relationship. The dynamics are actually very similar. Insights that are not sufficiently balanced by interest or rapture are not nourishing. The meditators have to stop straining, they need to return to the simplest of concentration practices and develop the balance and ease that grow naturally out of one-pointedness. The couples have to find a way to let each other become mysterious again. They, too, have to return to a simpler stance, before they knew everything there was to know about each other. In both cases, people have to let go of their fixed notions and return to a state of interest. A similar phenomenon afflicts some long-term veterans of psychotherapy. They can have deep insights into themselves but still be contracted, rigid, or unhappy. They lack the spirit that Freud evidently took for granted but that his followers neglected to encourage.

In an important article entitled "Psychoanalysis and the Degradation of Romance," psychoanalyst Stephen A. Mitchell argued that psychoanalysis long overlooked the critical importance of idealization and joy in people's lives. With its emphasis on rationality and accommodation, Mitchell said, psychoanalysis became unbalanced, promoting a picture of mature love that "often seems a somber, dispassionate affair, indistinguishable from mourning."[34] As it tended to do in other areas, psychoanalysis aligned itself with the disappointments of life instead of the potential for growth. By treating romance the way Freud did the oceanic feeling, as a remnant of some kind of infantile preoccupation, modern psychotherapists all too often support the notion that joy has little place in adult life. But, as Mitchell pointed out, the preservation of the capacity for joy depends on, and supports, the ability to tolerate surprise and unpredictability in one's life and one's partner. This is a Buddhist insight that has resurfaced in a psychoanalytic vein. Through the influence of therapists like Mitchell, psychotherapy has been struggling to correct its own imbalance. With its grounding in the Middle Path, Buddhism can prove to be an important influence in this correction.

In the classical Buddhist psychology, joy and rapture serve as the foundations for faith, energy, mindfulness, and concentration. They make successful introspection and relationship possible. They may not directly promote wisdom, but they create a climate of mind in which wisdom can flourish. They are not cultivated as an end in themselves but as the means of maintaining an environment that is supportive of investigation and freedom. Before I ever entered into a long-term psychotherapy of my own, I learned from meditation how to be with the entire range of my emotional experience, with the faith that joy and rapture were always within reach.

SUDDEN AWAKENING

One of my great teachers in this regard was Ram Dass, who, after my first summer at Naropa, continued to surface in my life in the role of teacher and guide. Upon my return to Massachusetts after Naropa, in the first flush of my encounter with Buddhism, I discovered that the psychology professor who had fired Ram Dass from Harvard after his LSD debacle, David McClelland, had, with his wife Mary, opened his house to a group of young spiritual seekers, many of whom had just returned with Ram Dass from India. In his public life David had repudiated him, but in his private life he had maintained and developed their connection.

The McClelland's yellow house, a comfortable, rambling, wooden structure on the top of the highest hill in Cambridge, became my second home. It felt like a stop on the underground railroad, with teachers and devotees of a variety of spiritual disciplines mingling with an eccentric assortment of psychologists, anthropologists, students, dropouts, and art historians, all drawn together by a growing interest in the wisdom of the East. There was meditation and chanting every Tuesday night, and whatever spiritual teachers were in town would inevitably be present. The first Tibetan lamas to travel to the United States all stayed there. David, one of the most respected members of the psychology department, who must have been sixty years old by then, would come down to the living room in his slippers and sit in the back. He reminded me of the great Greek King Milinda, who after conquering a swath of Buddhist India became a convert to the religion of his subjects. Ram Dass was a frequent visitor, and for several years in the late 1970s, he taught a group of us on weekend afternoons in the McClelland's carriage house.

Ram Dass had an infectious grounding in joy and rapture; his devotion to his recently deceased guru and his efforts to use everything in his life as a teaching had enabled him to cultivate these qualities with great success. In the classes that he led, he would use chanting, meditation, and various yogic techniques of breath control to focus and quiet our minds, and then he would use his stories and humor to delight us. But what I remember most clearly is how he used the concentrated awareness we created to help us look more deeply into our own selves. We would often meditate together in a large group, only to have him call out, in a sudden punctuation of the enveloping silence, "Mark (or Elliot or Perry), what have you got?" He was asking for a snapshot of our mental and physical experiences of the moment, a peek at our emotions. This demand, even if I could only partially meet it, required an attempt at honesty that felt like a stretch. I could sit silently in meditation with relative ease by this point, but to have to give a cross-section of my mind at some random point in front of the entire group was challenging. I noticed that even when he called on somebody else, I felt a jolt of awareness and a slowly emerging willingness to admit to whatever tangle of mind I was caught up in at the time. Needless to say, it became easy to tell, within the group, who was hiding behind bliss or peacefulness and who was willing to use those qualities to help examine themselves more openly.

This technique, of sudden awakening, was similar to another strategy that Ram Dass employed on a ten-day retreat that he led in those days. At this retreat, which, like others I had attended by then, required a mostly silent practice of concentrated awareness throughout the day, a bell would ring at three o'clock in the morning for a special middle-of-the-night meditation. I did not realize it at the time, but this was to be one of the best preparations I could ever have for being both a doctor and a parent, since the most difficult thing about both callings is being awakened in the middle of the night and having to put one's own needs aside. The three o'clock meditation required me to rise from a deep sleep and work with my immediate resistance to what was demanded. I was grumpy, tired, and irritable, but those meditations were also powerful celebrations. The stillness of the night was vast.

WORKING WITH REGRET

One of my discoveries in these periods of self-reflection was that I did not always find what I thought I should. I had the idea, for instance, that by excavating the facts, or the memories, of the past, I could be free of their emotional consequences. Yet this did not always turn out to be true. Often such understanding does not provide release. It gives an explanation, but we are still stuck with the results and, all too often, the persistent desire to change them. An autobiographical story from the Dalai Lama's recent *Art of Happiness* expressed this well. The story involved an elderly monk who regularly came to His Holiness for teachings, although the Dalai Lama considered him to be his superior in meditative attainment and would agree to teach him only as a kind of formality. On one occasion this monk asked the Dalai Lama for initiation into a particular set of demanding practices. The Dalai Lama demurred, saying that they were meant for younger monks, that they were vigorous and demanding exercises he wished to spare the man from undertaking. The next thing he knew, this monk committed suicide, hoping to be reborn into a younger body with better stamina. The Dalai Lama was asked by his interviewer and co-writer, an American psychiatrist, how he dealt with his regret, how he made it go away.

"It didn't go away," the Dalai Lama replied, a little perplexed by the question. "It is still there."

In the context in which it was originally presented, this story is powerful because of the mindset of the interviewer. It never occurred to him that the regret would not go away. It was interesting to see the Western psychiatrist assuming the reality of impermanence, while the Buddhist teacher asserted the lasting nature of his regret. Yet this was precisely what was so moving about the story. The psychiatrist was operating from the point of view of fixing the pain rather than feeling it. The Dalai Lama, for all his good humor, had the fortitude, and the faith, to accept his regret without looking to heal it. This is the essence of the Buddhist approach to psychological change. Striving to get rid of the pain only reinforces it, while acceptance of the truth deepens our capacity for tolerance, patience, and forgiveness. The Dalai Lama was forever changed by the loss of his friend and by his part in it. How could he not be?

In Buddhist psychology two mental factors, called shame and dread, are considered to be skillful qualities that increase with meditative awareness. When I first learned about them, I thought that there must be some mistake. How could shame and dread be *positive* qualities? Would we not want to free ourselves from them, as we do from anger or fear? But these mental factors are unique. Their function is to make us shrink from unskillful actions, to recognize the negative consequences of our deeds, and to develop a wariness toward repeating our mistakes. The Dalai Lama was honest enough with himself to recognize the role he had played, however unwittingly, in his friend's suicide, and to have regret over it. He did not attempt to rationalize the situation, to excuse himself, or to grieve his loss and move on. In the Buddhist view, all of these approaches would have involved cling-ing. This was why the Dalai Lama's admission was so startling. His idea of freedom was not necessarily the same as ours.

A recent experience with a patient illustrates a similar point. Patricia came to me in a period of extended but incompletely processed mourning for her father, who had died four years before. Divorced and now in her mid-forties, Patricia's grief was complicated. Not only had she lost her father through illness and death, but he had abandoned her and her mother when she was ten. Patricia had refused to see him after that, until close to the time of his death, when she allowed some rapprochement. For Patricia, love and abandonment became inextricably intertwined, and she resisted any kind of intimate attachments, except for rare encounters with people who were already heading out of town. Patricia had the idea that her love was tarnished, that it inevitably brought destruction or abandonment in its wake; she was on strike, waiting for the equation of love and loss to evap-orate. Privately, she seemed to feel that affection was only valid if it was childlike or unconflicted. More than anything, she wanted to get rid of the painful equation of love and death that had colored her life. My sense was that there was no going back, that her yearning for a more innocent time was like the American psychiatrist's wanting the Dalai Lama to give up his regret. But I also sensed that the painful associations that accompanied her loving feelings did not need to be an obstacle to intimacy. Hers was a love that could embrace heartbreak.

Patricia had a great deal of trouble with her positive feelings for me, since she expected that they would in some way drive me away, alienate me, or destroy me. This is not unusual in psychotherapy; it can be a self-fulfilling prophecy, since the free expression of eroticized love between patient and therapist can indeed wreak havoc with the relationship. So my task was once again to steer a middle path, to accept her affection without indulging it, while acknowledging the links between love and abandonment that were so real to Patricia.

There was something in my Buddhist training that affected the way I related to Patricia, something that allowed me to accept the reality of her pos-itive feelings without merely reducing them to the psychoanalytic concept of transference, in which unfinished emotions from childhood are thought to be played out in the relationship with the therapist. Just as joy and rapture are the natural expressions of a mind that is relaxed in concentrated awareness, affection and trust are the natural expressions of a person who is "met" in psychotherapy. It is the foundation upon which the relationship is built.

In Patricia's case this natural expression was tarnished by her early experience. She was at once hopeful and deeply pessimistic when she felt herself becoming attached to me. She both wanted and resented me and felt pulled into the relationship as if against her will. She was caught in an oppressive dilemma. On the one hand, she clung to the somewhat magical belief that I had the power to free her from the pain of her past. She wanted therapy to lobotomize her or to erase her memory, just as she wanted it to take her over and fill her life. And then, upon finding that all this was impossible, she would swing to the opposite extreme of bitterness, disillusionment, and frustration. She felt that she did not matter at all, that our relationship was a false one, and that there was nothing genuine between us. Like the psychoanalysts' forsaking of romance, or Freud's paralysis in analysis, she was an idealist who easily became a nihilist. Like Sona the lute player in the Buddha's original teachings, she tuned our relationship (the instrument of our work) either too taut or too loose.

My effort with Patricia was to use her positive feelings as a canvas upon which to paint the incomplete feelings of her traumatic loss of her father. She was surprised at the depth and intensity of her attachment to me, and she expected our relationship to replicate the one with her father. In some way, she believed in transference more than I did. She assumed that she would drive me away, that her neediness or dependency would lead me to abandon her. This was not some unconscious fantasy that I had to interpret for her; it was what she consciously believed, and, in a perverse way, what she wanted. My job was to outlast her attempts at destruction, to survive both her desire and her hostility. Just as I had to learn, as a parent, not to react personally to my children's anger at me, so with Patricia did I have to maintain my presence undistractedly. I had to be able to respond authentically while not reacting. No matter how hard she tried to make me into her father, I had to remain myself.

It may sound peculiar that the core of a Buddhist therapy was the effort to hold on to my individuality, but that is often the case. Patricia was intent on putting me into a box rather than letting me be, but I was able to hold on. I came to believe that she wanted me to act like her father so that she would not have to own what had already happened with him. As Freud deduced early on, many people prefer to act out what they refuse to completely remember.

For a long time Patricia resisted my efforts. She reminded me of the Buddha as he wrestled with his memory of the rose-apple tree. Full of penance, she was afraid of the pleasure that leapt out of the shadows, the pleasure that did not depend on sensory gratification but that came naturally to our relationship. But unlike the Buddha, she did not give up her fear so easily. She kept trying to turn her positive feelings into a problem, or into an attachment. But I knew that their true nature was no problem. My confidence in this allowed her to gradually settle down. Her dreams began to contain vivid reminders of her father's departure and subsequent death. She let herself get involved with a man who was not moving away. And her trust in the "going on" nature of our relationship deepened. In allowing our instrument to be just as it was, she found that it had a wonderful sound and was easily playable.

CHAPTER 10

BUDDHA'S MEDICINE

A s my meditation developed, I began to get into the swing of things. Feelings of joy or elation no longer seemed so unusual, and I became able to peer more intensely into my own mind. Out of nowhere, strange snippets of verse sometimes appeared. "Nowhere to run to, nowhere to hide," I heard emerging out of the shadows of my mind one evening, quieted by days of meditation practice. Bits of song lyrics often wafted up to chronicle my insights. Old sounds from the radio seemed to call from the distance. "It's been a long time coming," I remember hearing early one morning while on retreat, "It's going to be a long time gone."

My understanding of what I was doing in meditation began to undergo a subtle but important shift. At first I imagined that I was engaged in something akin to a battle, an ever-deepening, ever-opening confrontation with the way things are. Obstacles to peace of mind were everywhere, from the chattering of my thinking to the intensity of my emotions to the rustling of the person next to me. I thought at first that I had to conquer them all. But as I began to appreciate how small a chance I had of winning such a battle (reality was bigger than I was), I shifted my approach. Confrontation was too confrontational; I needed something more akin to engagement: a deepening appreciation of reality, a co-mingling with it, a dissolving into, perhaps even a oneness with, this fabric of life such that the world began to appear, not as an obstacle, but as a vast tapestry of which I was but a single stitch. As I explored that tapestry, it began to seem increasingly ephemeral, making the words of the Diamond Sutra come alive in a new way. The world, says this sutra, is but "a star at dawn, a bubble in a stream, a flash of lightning in a summer cloud, a flickering lamp, a phantom, and a dream." The closer I looked at things, the less solid they appeared. The fabric of life had great tenacity, but it could also seem very sheer.

THE DAWNING OF INSIGHT

In the classical psychology of Buddhism, the dawning of insight is said to be a terrifying time. In the place of a relatively secure world-view, every-thing suddenly looks shattered. The catalyst for this is the sudden realiza-tion that the mind's experience is self-perpetuating. By this I mean that it unfolds all by itself, without anyone behind it. Joseph Goldstein used to repeat the phrase "Empty phenomena rolling on," to connote this sense of ongoing anonymity. It is a difficult point to get across, until it jumps up and hits you over the head. Usually we are so identified with thoughts, feelings, and experiences that it would never occur to us to see things differently. But it is an unmistakable consequence of mindfulness meditation that we start to notice that we are no longer necessary. Thoughts, feelings, emotions, and reactions all arise of their own accord. It is quite possible to notice them without identifying with their content, which is a strange and awesome experience, akin to watching waves pounding against the shore in antici-pation of a big storm. They just keep on coming. The original Pali word for a Buddhist monk, bhikkhu, means "fear seer," one who can tolerate his own terror. At the point in meditation where the first glimpse of lack of identity is realized, this terror can become quite pronounced. In Zen Buddhism it is compared to an open-eyed man falling backward into a well.

When the powers of perception are sharpened and the mind is quieted, thoughts can be observed from their inception. Usually we notice thinking somewhere down the line of a train of associations—we catch ourselves "lost in thought." But at certain times in meditation we can observe a thought just as it is forming, just as it is bursting into consciousness. This is a very strange experience at first, for it immediately begs the question "Who is thinking?" The thoughts appear to come from nowhere, and the tendency to identify one-self as the thinker of those thoughts is loosened. The thoughts just come and go, artifacts of some mysterious process that we ourselves are also a part of.

DEATH IS EVERYWHERE

In the stability of meditation, first the arising and then the passing away of these thoughts (or feelings) become more interesting than their content. The more we examine them, the more their ephemeral nature captures our attention. It can start to be something like a fireworks display. In a moment-to-moment way, we see creation and destruction, all within the theater of the mind. At a certain point, usually the time of greatest terror, the passing away takes center stage. All formations keep on literally breaking up. Like scenes in the movie *Groundhog Day*, the same phenomena repeat themselves. As the Buddhist texts describe it, "Like fragile pottery being smashed, like fine dust being dispersed, like sesame seeds being roasted," the phenomena of the world keep on dissolving.

While this might sound like a bad dream, or some kind of drug-induced altered state of consciousness, in the view of Buddhist psychologists this is the true state of the world. All phenomena *are* constantly in upheaval; rather than being fixed entities, they are consistently coming and going. As the powers of perception are developed, this reality comes more and more into focus. According to the *Visuddhimagga*, the classical textbook of Buddhist psychology, this period of meditation is like standing on the bank of a river during a heavy rain while large bubbles appear on the surface of the water, only to see them pop as quickly as they appear. "Formations," the meditator begins to realize, "break up all the time."[35] The image that is used to describe this stage of meditation is one of a sage with a burning turban; the volatile nature of reality is literally upon him.

The best metaphor that I ever found to describe this view of the nature of reality came from a fellow student at Harvard who refused to write a paper for a psychology course we were taking from Daniel Goleman, and insisted instead on building a model of consciousness. My friend, Michael Feldman, whom I had long considered to be a brilliant but idiosyncratic thinker, created his project in a sudden burst of energy. I had no idea what he was up to and was worried about him failing the course. He found a bicycle wheel somewhere and mounted it so that it could spin freely, looking something like a sculpture by Marcel Duchamp. He then took broken pieces of mirror and attached one piece to each spoke of the wheel. When the wheel was spun fast enough, the pieces of mirror coalesced into a single unit and the spinning mirror wheel gave a perfect reflection of whatever it was facing. But if the wheel was turned just a little more slowly, the individual images could be seen flickering in a staccato-like manner, as if rapidly blinking on and off. It was the perfect three-dimensional representation of the moment-to-moment nature of consciousness, showing how the same mechanism could give both a unified and a fractured view of reality.

In Buddhist meditation there comes a time when the mind is able to tolerate a direct peek at reality. Rather than operating under the influence of ignorance, mistaking the image in the mirror for truth, the mind is able to see through the mirror's reflection, into the substrate of arising and passing away. What once had seemed so solid, comforting, and desirable now appears as nothing but trouble. Wherever a meditator turns, he finds only more dissolution. Death is everywhere. There is a description of this in the *Visuddhimagga* that I have always loved, because of its imagery of no escape. The dawning of insight, it is said, means that the world is experienced "in the form of a great terror," the way "lions, tigers, leopards, bears, hyenas, spirits, ogres, fierce bulls, savage dogs, rut-maddened wild elephants, hideous venomous serpents, thunderbolts, charnel grounds, battlefields, flaming coal pits, etc., appear to a timid man who wants to live in peace."[36] If nothing is lasting or stable then all is insubstantial. This is what is meant by the word "groundlessness," which is often used to describe the Buddha's insight. Out of this vision of groundlessness comes not resignation but a kind of benevolent acceptance, a profound equanimity that understands and accepts the essential instability of all things.

One of the consequences is that our perception of death changes. If things do not exist as fixed, independent entities, then how can they die? Our notion of death as the sudden expiration of that which was once so real starts to unwind. When things are perceived to be flickering rather than static, we no longer fear their demise in quite the same way. We may fear their instability, or their emptiness, but the looming threat of death starts to seem absurd. Things are constantly dying, we find. Or rather, they are constantly in flux, arising and passing away with each moment of consciousness.

There is a tale in the classical tradition of Buddhism about a group of thirty monks who, upon receiving meditation instruction from the Buddha, went into retreat during the rainy season in a remote forest dwelling. Enthusiastic in their practice, they resolved to meditate in isolation from each other and to stay awake throughout the three watches of the night as best they could. But unbeknownst to them a tiger roamed their forest, waiting until the early morning when one of the monks would sleepily nod off to swoop down and carry him off for supper. Fifteen monks were plucked by the tiger in this way, without one of them even having the chance to call for help. Finally the remaining bhikkhus, in a hastily arranged conference, agreed to make every effort to yell out to each other should the tiger reappear. The next monk to be seized did indeed manage to alert the others, and the remaining bhikkhus came running with sticks and torches. The tiger, however, dragged the young monk to a rocky promontory that was inaccessible to the men and began to eat his prize from the feet upward. They called out to him that there was nothing to be done and that now was the time to put his meditation to work. Even in death his effort went toward not being lost in reactions. Prostrate in the tiger's mouth, the monk "suppressed his pain" and began to develop insight into the insubstantial nature of his own body and mind. His demise was another opportunity to go on being. The monk's death poem is quoted as follows:

> *Virtuous was I keeping to my vows*
> *And wise with growing insight was my mind*
> *That had to concentration well attained.*
> *Yet, because I slacked for just a while,*
> *A tiger took my frame of flesh and blood,*
> *Unto a hill and then my mind did quake.*
> *Devour me as you please, O tiger, eat*
> *This body of mine which is bereft of thought;*
> *Within the thought of quiet strongly held*
> *A blessing will my death become to me.*[37]

This is a famous story in Buddhist countries dating from the earliest writ-ten Southeast Asian commentaries. In Tibet, whose Buddhist heritage is rooted in the earlier traditions of medieval India but which evolved its own Buddhist culture some fifteen hundred years after the Buddha, there devel-oped a further elaboration of this story. "Don't feed yourself to the first tiger that comes along," they warn their yogis. Just because you understand that death is not to be feared does not mean that you should throw your life away, even to feed a hungry predator.

Yet for me, the power of the story is not just in the young monk's ability to surrender to his fate; it is in the way it evokes the powerlessness that we all have in the face of death. We never know when it is going to swoop down and take us, nor what form it will be in. It might be cancer or diabetes or a stroke in lieu of a tiger, but the outcome will be the same. Like the young monk we may be witness to our own destruction, watching the steady progression as first one part of our body is devoured and then another. The monk's ability to surrender to the tiger seems extreme—we want him to fight and escape—but how different is it going to be for each of us?

SCARING DEATH INTO SUBMISSION

The first person I ever saw confront death was like the young monk in the story of the tiger. Her surrender made a lasting impression on me, not to be replicated until I stood by as my own therapist died slowly of bladder cancer many years later. When I was living in Massachusetts and going to medical school in the years after Naropa, meditating with Jack and Joseph on retreat and with Ram Dass at the McClelland's house during the rest of the year, death swooped down and slowly took David McClelland's wife, Mary.

Mary was the heart of my entire spiritual universe at the time. She was a Quaker, and a painter, and the one who had opened the McClelland's home to all the young seekers back from India. She was basically presid-ing over a commune and making possible weekly meditations for the larger community as well. For a number of years she had been painting large, haunting, blue surrealistic canvases filled with eerie imagery of bones and fish scales and deserts and light. She hung these paintings, one by one, in her living room, where we gathered every week to sing or meditate together. They seemed to emit a distant and ethereal glow. Then one day she got stomach cancer. In the midst of the burgeoning joy of her household, she got stomach cancer. Slowly over the next several years her appetite diminished, and she began to fade away, with her blue eyes growing ever more luminous. She and David shared their bed until the end, and our weekly meditations sometimes shifted from the living room to their bedroom. What has stayed with me is the way that joy and sorrow coexisted in the house for that time. I think this was because Mary was a true bhikkhu, a true fear seer. She was not afraid of her own fear, even as death sat upon her head like a burning turban.

In the Tibetan Buddhist tradition, where ornate visual representations of Buddhist insights were established or elaborated, this transformation in the understanding of death is symbolized by one of fiercest deities of the Tibetan archetypical pantheon. There is a figure called Yamantaka, the death destroyer, who is said to be the form adopted by the bodhisattva of wisdom, Manjushri, to conquer Yama, the Lord of Death. Manjushri's idea was to assume a form more frightening than death itself, capable of scaring death into submission, of showing death its ultimate unreality. Rather than allowing death to put an end to being, Manjushri's aim was to expose the illusory nature of the fear of death. Yamantaka's iconography was recently explained by the Buddhist scholar Robert A. F. Thurman, who carefully unpacked all of the symbolic meanings of what at first seems to be overpowering imagery. The deity is certainly awesome. With nine leering, blue-black buffalo heads, each with three eyes, and with thirty-four arms, two fire-spouting horns, a halo of flames arising from his burning hair, a headdress of skulls, and a perpetually erect phallus, Yamantaka is nothing if not a nightmare. Yet sprouting from his central head and rising toward the sky are two more heads: one a red, fanged demon face with diaphanous skin oozing blood; and the other the golden, shining, eternally youthful and handsome Manjushri, the bodhisattva of transcendent wisdom, an oasis of understanding in the midst of death's horror.

The story of Yamantaka is that Manjushri decided to tame death by assuming this intimidating form and simultaneously creating a huge mirror that magnified and reflected death's horrible appearance back to him, using death's own face to frighten and subdue him. This is consistent with the most basic Buddhist meditative approach: To stare something straight in the face is the best way to bring it under control. As Thurman put it, Manjushri trapped death "in the endless terror of eventually being killed himself." Manjushri caught death in the habit of imagining things to have an inherent and fixed reality, turned that thought habit back on him, and then used the resultant fear to bring him into submission. After paralyzing death in this way, the bodhisattva showed him the way out of his terror, revealing to the demon the transparency and interconnectedness of life, dissolving "the absolute severance death is imagined to be."[38]

Mary's death was as powerful for me as a vision of Yamantaka. Like golden Manjushri peeking out of the horrible form of the death destroyer, Mary's love burned all the brighter as she dissolved. Her death made an indelible impression on me, all the more so because it came at the time of completion of my medical education, just as I was to begin caring for sick and dying patients in a hospital in the Boston area.

BEING AND NON-BEING

As a psychiatrist in training, I was expected to do a one-year medical internship. I chose a program in a chronic care facility where there were wards of people who were not expected to recover from their illnesses. There was also a functioning intensive care unit and a locked prison ward serving the state's incarcerated population. It was a backwater hospital, for patients whom the medical establishment had little interest in, but it was also a place where friends of mine were establishing a short-lived "pain and stress" clinic with a natural foods kitchen and acupuncture in the outpatient clinic. The hospital was happy to have me: I was a doctor who spoke English and had gone to an American medical school, a rarity in that environment. The fact that I wanted to be a psychiatrist was not a liability.

My patients were not like Mary. I remember the first two people I ever cared for, both lying in their hospital beds suffering from illnesses that we could do nothing about. Mr. Fishman, a round and once overweight Jewish grocer, was gradually suffocating from emphysema, in which his lungs, made brittle from years of smoking, could no longer expand and contract to allow a flow of oxygen into his blood. He would gasp and call out to me, "Dr. Epstein, Dr. Epstein," whenever I was near, with the unquenched neediness of a hungry child. He was scared, and there was not much I could do for him. Mr. Houlihan, an alcoholic Irish shipyard worker, was shriveling up from chronic cirrhosis. His liver was shutting down and was unable to clear his blood of impurities. His skin and eyes were yellowing, he itched unrelievedly, and his belly was swollen with ascites, fluid that could no longer pass through the liver. He was withdrawn, turned over in his bed away from visitors and turned into himself, hardly looking up at his grown daughter who sometimes attended his bedside.

With both people I eventually adopted the strategy of just sitting with them for a bit every day. There was not really room for this in my schedule, but I would try to find time. Luckily my internship was not as frantic as most. I would think of Mary, or of the Diamond Sutra, or of the vision that death is happening all the time, to each of us; that it is not an unnatural thing. I would remember the terror of dissolution in meditation and the equanimity that came from not fighting it. I could not talk about any of this to my patients—I am sure it would not have been well received if I had—but I could stop and hang out just a bit. This was not the usual modus operandi on the hospital floor.

In some ways I could see myself in both Mr. Fishman and Mr. Houlihan. When the Buddha taught, in his Second Noble Truth, that the cause of suffering was "thirst" or "craving," he suggested that this thirst was of three types: the craving for sensory pleasures, the craving for being, and the craving for nonbeing. Craving for being meant the desire for more of what one already has. If only my wife could be more loving, if only the sunset could last longer, if only my best friend still lived around the corner. If only I felt as real as I was supposed to. Craving for nonbeing meant seeking oblivion, nothingness, the peace of deepest sleep, the hope that a problem could be eliminated altogether or that there was somewhere to escape to. One recent patient of mine described it as a craving for amputation, the wish that an obstacle could be cut off and thrown away or that the self could shrink down to nothing, withdrawing as far as possible into a cocoon of invisibility.

Mr. Fishman and Mr. Houlihan seemed to embody these two cravings. In their symptoms they were expressing a deeper pattern of behavior that ran through the texture of their lives. In his gasping after the next breath, Mr. Fishman was grasping for more of what he already had—oxygen—but in his anxiety he was using up that which was so precious to him. He would become increasingly short of breath the more he struggled. Mr. Houlihan was seeking the oblivion that he thought death could be, much as he had sought it through alcohol in his drinking days. He was not open to the life that remained for him, embodied in the presence of his daughter at his side.

In sitting quietly with each of these men, I did not do therapy, nor did I meditate. I simply sat with them, aware of the continuity of their going on being. They were so caught up in their dying that they were no longer very available. I attempted to use my presence to give them something to focus on, without feeling sorry for them and without pushing them away. I wanted them to know themselves as spirit, as something more than their ailing minds and bodies. I do not have any real way of knowing how successful I was at communicating any of this, but I do know that they both liked me. Mr. Fishman calmed down a bit, and Mr. Houlihan opened up a little. There were moments when I felt that each was a bit less afraid, when my awareness touched the place in them that was beyond craving. Although I did not know it at the time, I can see now that these men were among my earliest teachers in psychotherapy. With each of them, unable to help them in more conventional ways, I had to become a fear seer.

The danger of this particular stance, or at least of my expression of it, is that it can sometimes be too cool, too much observation without enough participation. This is why, in the Buddhist view, insight without compassion is thought to be heartless. To truly appreciate the ephemeral nature of things is to realize that we are all in the same boat, even though it may not be my turn to be eaten by the tiger. When my wife had our first baby, for example, I was with her throughout her labor, but she found me unhelpful in the times of most duress because of my belief that her awareness could somehow contain the pain that she was experiencing. I was attached to the notion of observing with equanimity, and this kept me apart, at times, from the actual experience. When she was in labor with our second child, I threw all that away and was just there with her. I gave her my body to hold on to or to push against. I remember her screaming and pulling on the hair of my head until I thought she would pull it all out, her pain was so intense. But we had a wonderful birth, in which we were all transformed. With my first patients, before I had assumed much of a professional identity, I think I was able to be present with them without that subtle sense of distancing. As I have worked more, I have had to keep undercutting my professional stance in order not to lose the person-to-person contact that makes awareness so powerful.

Birth and death are fruitful in the manner in which they undercut the complacency of who we think we are, in the way in which they shake us up and make us question ourselves. If we let them, they can strip away the layers of identity that imprison us, exposing us to the groundlessness that is the bedrock of the Buddha's vision. Like my early patients in the hospital, we often try to protect ourselves from the enormity of that vision, imagining it to be too terrifying to tolerate. My response to our first childbirth experience had that same protective clinging in it—I was trying to hold on to my observing stance as a bulwark against the raw terror, and excitement, of my daughter's birth and my wife's pain. But hearts and minds open when we can allow ourselves to be swept away by such experiences.

The Buddha consistently recommended this approach to his followers, right down to the moment of his own death. His insight meditations were always about opening the mind to the relentless flow that underlies our consensual realities. Over and over again, he encouraged his monks to tune in to the dissolution of everything that they held so dear, not to depress them but to let them love more completely, free from attachment to that which is inherently insubstantial. "Indeed bhikkhus," he said to them, an old man on the verge of his final breath, "I declare this to you: It is in the nature of all formations to dissolve. Attain perfection through diligence."[39] The Buddha's final words distilled his vision down to the bone, even as, in his death, he became a living embodiment of what he was preaching.

THE EYE OF THE STORM

It may sound odd, but one of my greatest teachings about all of this came in the middle of a girl's softball game that my eleven-year-old daughter was pitching. It was a pick-up game with the parents, since the opposing girls' team had failed to show up for the scheduled event, and I was playing a shallow right field, while my daughter was on the pitcher's mound. She was a good, consistent pitcher, lobbing the ball underhand to the opposing hitters. The third batter, one of the grown-ups, was hitting left-handed so as not to hit the ball too deep, but on his first swing he cracked the ball straight back to the mound into my daughter's face. She bent forward, hands and glove over her cheekbones, and then reared back and screamed to the sky, her nose spouting blood like a fountain. I raced toward her, but the world had clicked into slow motion. I couldn't reach her fast enough, and it seemed as if no one else was moving at all, like one of those episodes of *The Twilight Zone* where everything freezes. My daughter reminded me of the great Hindu goddess Kali, queen of destruction, whose bloody mouth and necklace of severed heads signify her role as destroyer of illusion. Her screams circled my head like a pack of vultures. When I finally reached her, I cradled her in my arms and carried her off the field. Parents and children surrounded us, and we managed to staunch the flow of blood with somebody's shirt. I probed her face with my fingers to look for broken bones and felt a reassuring firmness to my pressure. She was quite still in my arms, weeping softly. Another parent whispered to me that her nose was probably broken. Someone fetched my car and we carried her to it, my eight-year-old son toting the bloody glove and trailing quietly behind.

The curious thing was the peace we all felt. It was an anxious peace, to be sure, but it was strangely calm. Our world had been fractured, but we were all still together, perhaps even more so. Our car felt like a boat, as we wove our way home, big and wide. My daughter was moaning that she wished she were dead, but said later she just couldn't think of anything else to say. I got her home and placed her on the yellow couch with ice on her nose and called the pediatrician. I examined her again under the doctor's instruction and decided that nothing seemed broken. The pediatrician told me what to watch out for but determined that we did not have to rush to the emergency room. There was not much else to do, other than wait for Mom to come home.

As in a deep meditation, the sudden perception of destruction had jolted us all into another kind of consciousness. When my wife walked into the house, my daughter took pleasure in her mother's horrified, and loving, response. She had looked over the precipice and survived, with two black eyes and a swollen face to show for it. When both kids had to write auto-biographical pieces for school the next fall, each one wrote about what had happened. "What I learned from this," my son wrote, in a phrase that my daughter appropriated for her essay as well, "is that a softball is not soft." Things are not what they seem, we all realized for an instant. The tiger can swoop down at any time. I did not say it to them, but to myself I repeated a somewhat different moral. The world plays hardball with us, I thought, and we are not in charge. It is the nature of formations to dissolve.

But we did not emerge from this with more fear, we came out of it with more confidence. It was not fragility that made such an impact, it was our ability to meet it. In the midst of the dissolution of things as we knew them, some sort of acceptance took hold, and it arose spontaneously. Our instinctive surrender permitted us to be totally present, come what may. There is a certain kind of confidence that precipitates out of these crises, the faith in our own capacity to face that which we most dread. I still do not know where such calm comes from, but I am more willing to believe that I have not seen the last of it.

When I was in medical school, I sought out a professor of psychiatry named Robert Coles to supervise me in an independent study. Coles was an anomaly at Harvard Medical School, a humanist with an avowed interest in religion who was known for his prize-winning writings on the spiritual, emotional, and ethical lives of children. He taught electives in the medical humanities that were generally offered to medical students in January, when other more rigorous courses were in hibernation. Because I was one of the only students heading for a career in psychiatry, Coles was willing to supervise me. I wanted to read about the existential movement in psychotherapy. I was aware of the comments of Binswanger about the need for more spirit in psychoanalysis, and I was hoping that I might find links within existential thought to the psychology of Buddhism that had already captivated my interest.

I met with Coles in his book-lined study at Harvard College, across the river and a world away from the hospital-based medical school where I spent most of my time. It was an unusual and pleasant interlude for me. Coles was casual and informal in his manner; dressed in his trademark sweater and corduroys, he had the air of the rumpled intellectual, a one-time adviser to Bobby Kennedy. He was curious about me, and I could see how his ease and charm worked to his benefit as a psychotherapist. He drew out my family history, questioning me about my parents and their relationship to my spiritual interests. I could see him looking at me with a mix of fascination and suspicion. I was clearly the first medical student with an interest in Buddhism to cross his path.

Coles agreed to supervise me and was happy to let me do pretty much whatever I wanted. He was busy and I was self-directed, so we were a good match. But he did insist that I read some things he recommended that did not fall directly under the rubric of the existentialists. He wanted me to know some of the work of Freud's daughter, Anna, especially her volume called *War and Children*, a record of her efforts during the Second World War to care for the emotional needs of displaced and traumatized British young people. I think he wanted me to see an engaged psychoanalyst, one capable of bringing her understanding to the sufferings of real life. He also was the first to mention Winnicott to me, although I did not follow up until some years later. And he told me to look at the writings of a psychoanalyst and social critic named Allen Wheelis, whose books, *The Quest for Identity* and *How People Change*, I managed to find. I believe Coles was responding to my psychological emptiness, as well as to my ambivalence about psycho-analysis, for Wheelis's thesis seemed to be that accelerating social change had undermined traditional identities, leaving people lost and in search of themselves. Wheelis made the point that identity could not be uncovered through the analysis of instincts, only instincts could be uncovered that way. The contemporary self was not so much lost as outgrown, he felt, because of changing social mores and expectations. If identity was not lost, then it could not very well be found. It could only be created afresh. In this way he was very much of an existentialist, indeed.

Wheelis stressed how awareness of old patterns of reactivity created more choice for an individual. He even used the word "freedom." He crit-icized psychoanalysis for proposing that people change simply by uncov-ering unconscious fears, impulses, defenses, and anxieties, and he recognized that this kind of analysis often leaves people feeling even more powerless, victims of forces over which they have no control. But Wheelis still sounded depressed. He seemed to have nothing else to fall back on, other than the hope that "man" could become more of his own creator. The radiant Buddha mind that underlies our conventional selves was nowhere to be found in his vision.

Somewhere in Wheelis's book he made the startling statement that "free-dom depends on awareness."[40] In this I could not be more in agreement. But

Wheelis did not have an experience of how liberating awareness could actually be. He did not seem to know that awareness could be cultivated, nor that it could be deployed on feelings of nothingness *and* on the tendency to identify with thoughts. In my own investigation of Buddhist meditation, I have seen how it is possible to change, not by making my problems go away or even by exploring them more deeply, but by cultivating my capacity to accept things as they are. Unlike what Dr. Wheelis thought, my identity *was* lost, and social change was not the culprit. When I learned to restrain my own patterns of reactivity, my identity had a chance to reveal itself, not as a fixed entity but as flow and potential. Meditation has enabled me to take possession of myself, to inhabit myself, not through identification but through acceptance.

As I began to work as a psychotherapist, I knew that this was the key to change. The obstacles that prevent us from living in a fully aware state must be brought into consciousness. The most pernicious of these obstacles is the sense of psychological emptiness, self-estrangement that often takes the form of unworthiness, low self-esteem, feelings of unreality, dissociation, shame, or self-hatred. In the writings of D. W. Winnicott is a model consistent with Buddhist teachings, one that enables a translation of Buddhism into the language of psychology.

As Winnicott described it, the investigation of early childhood experience is important, not just as a window into unconscious drives, but as an explanation for how the reactive patterns that obscure our true selves were established. Children who are forced to cope with intrusive or ignoring parental figures develop a compensatory self that manages their parents' needs or neglect. This self develops out of a need for survival, but the price that is paid is a high one. The child's own going on being is sacrificed, and the child loses confidence in himself or herself. Falseness and unreality replace aliveness and vitality.

Meditation is the Buddha's medicine. The mind is trained through restraint not to interfere or abandon. Patience, acceptance, and trust are encouraged, while the meditator is cautioned not to push away the unpleasant or hold on to the pleasant. The reactive mind gives way to a vast holding capacity out of which insight comes.

It is the knowledge of this ability to retrain the mind that has been lack-ing in Western psychology. There is no reason that the interpersonal vehi-cle of psychotherapy cannot be as effective in encouraging it as the intrapersonal one of meditation, but we have to recognize the potential. Psychotherapy can be enormously helpful in pointing out a person's habit-ual reactive patterns as they occur in the here-and-now. The therapeutic relationship itself is a powerful vehicle because of its intrinsic non-intrusive and non-abandoning nature. But the most important element, as the Buddha discovered, is the healing power of awareness. In the ancient Buddhist psychology of Abhidharma there are a host of odd-sounding "mental factors" that become strengthened by meditative absorption. They have such names as buoyancy, pliancy, adaptability, and proficiency. As a meditator reclaims the platform of joy and rapture, these abilities start to assert themselves. They are enablers of the capacity to go on being, balm for the mind, since they permit an individual to find balance in a sea of change. No longer struggling to find certainty in an endlessly shifting real-ity, a person grounded in awareness is free to discover and declare herself afresh as life unfolds. In the somewhat awkward language of psychody-namics, we call this the ability to live in an uninterrupted flow of authen-tic self.

MEDITATION IN ACTION

I had an experience not long ago in the unlikely venue of a neighborhood yoga class that seemed to wrap all of this up for me. The yoga class was just beginning, and I had not been coming for very long. I was pretty much in my own world and concerned with getting myself set up properly. The class was a little late getting started, and we were all lined up expectantly, if a bit restlessly, on our sticky blue mats, like overgrown preschoolers at nap time. Ready with blocks, blankets, and belts, we waited for the new teacher to gather himself into his leading role. I was fond of this before-the-beginning beginning; it was a between state, a *bardo*, a passageway from one world to the next. Dressed in our yoga clothes we could be anybody, or nobody, but we were unmistakably ourselves. I could not even see very well, having left my glasses and keys carefully askew in my shoes at the back of the dusty Manhattan studio where the yoga class takes place.

The feeling in the room was anxious but cautiously optimistic, as it is in the therapy office when a new but eager patient has just come in, before she has told me much of her story. I liked this period because of how brief but unstructured it was; it never went on long enough for me get too uncomfortable but it gave me a needed respite from the rest of my busy day. As when flying between cities in an airplane, I was suspended for a time. The remnants of my outside life could settle down before the tasks of this inside practice took over.

I do not intend this to be mean, but I was taken aback by what happened next. (The unconscious knows no negatives, I was taught when studying Freud. If someone tells me they are not upset, I know they probably are.) Actually, nothing out of the ordinary really happened. The new yoga teacher sat down in the front of the class and took a deep breath. He told us to sit up straight and close our eyes. He sang a simple Sanskrit mantra and asked us to chant it back to him. It was not an unfamiliar mantra, but something in his tone disturbed my reverie. What was it, I wondered? He was only chanting "Om," for goodness sake. But something else was coming through the sound, an insistent quality, not quite a demand but an expectation. I felt a wall going up around me, and noticed that he got a tepid response from the class. We were no longer in the between but were suddenly somewhere that no one seemed motivated to be. "It's not just me," I consoled myself; other people had also contracted. He continued, bravely, but his song had more of that unrelenting tone. He wanted something from us, all right. It was there in his voice. It was like being with a mother who was too anxious for us to eat. Our own going on being was interrupted as we mobilized to deal with the teacher's needs.

He only repeated the mantra three times; the whole thing was not a big deal. It would have been nice if we had all come around and started to sing and turned it into something positive, a big exhalation, but we did not do so. A few people ventured a response. I did not give much of one. I thought back to another teacher's chanting, though. Her class was the first I ever attended, and her singing, too, caught me off-guard; it had never occurred to me that there would be chanting before a lunchtime yoga class. But Julie's voice had astonished me. She sang quietly and beautifully as if to herself, very briefly at the start of class, a prayer or an invocation to let us begin. If my mind were a candle, her chanting would not have caused a flutter. Julie was pregnant, I found out subsequently, so perhaps she was not singing just to herself after all. Nevertheless, whomever she was singing to, it did not cause waves in the class.

This teacher was a different story. Were my mind a candle, it would have been blown out. His agenda filled the room, and we were suddenly pulled inside of it, as if a big vacuum had opened and sucked us all up. Like a stowaway in a packing crate in the hold of an ocean freighter, I was trapped in the bubble of another's desire.

I thought right away of a patient of mine, a psychologist-in-training who was doing his internship while seeing me in therapy. Jim was a brilliant therapist, but all too eager to share his insights with his patients. A student of meditation, he was aware of how his eagerness interfered with his effectiveness. His patients tended to experience him as telling them what to think instead of helping them come to their senses. "I feel like I'm always trying too hard to be effective, like I'm doing some sort of a job," he would say, well aware of the irony of his words. He was doing a job, of course, but it was not a job that required action. (A Taoist might say it was a job that required non-action.) With his typical therapeutic acumen, he was able to see where his zeal came from. "I'm trying to overcome a core sense of inadequacy," he told me off-handedly one day. His enthusiasm had a compensatory quality that turned his patients off, even when what he had to say was technically correct. There was something of this in my yoga teacher, as well. We all knew that he wanted a rousing introduction to his class, that he wanted to take us higher. But in reaching for it his personality became all figure and no ground.

As I continue to take classes with my yoga teacher, I can see how much he wants to create a spiritual environment for us. While his intention is noble, our yoga postures are burdened by his desire for them to be special. His class provides a special challenge, one that I did not bargain for at the beginning. It recapitulates an all-too-familiar childhood drama, in which parental expectations can overwhelm a child's burgeoning self-expression. But I have come to look forward to it as a unique form of therapy, one in which I can practice being free while restrained by the mind of another. It is the converse of what I try to do as a therapist, but it is the true test of what I have learned.

ACKNOWLEDGMENTS

This book had its genesis in a trip to Devon, England, where Stephen Batchelor had arranged a conference on Buddhism in contemporary culture. While staying in Devon, I asked Stephen if he knew a story about the Buddha's childhood memory of watching his father work in the fields. He showed me Bhikkhu Nanamoli's *Life of the Buddha*, and we located the vignette. Informal conversations at that conference with Stephen, his wife, Martine, and Francisco Varela confirmed for me the viability of writing about how people change. Reading Michael Eigen's recently published work *The Psychoanalytic Mystic* on the plane ride home filled me with inspiration for the task, as did subsequent discussions with him over dinner. Several presentations with Robert Thurman and Sharon Salzberg at Tibet House in New York allowed me to try out and refine these ideas, and Bob and Sharon's responses, feedback, and ideas helped shape this book. Their wisdom and compassion shine through my words.

Conversation with Ram Dass at his home in Marin County similarly inspired and focused me. Joseph Goldstein and Jack Kornfield kindly reviewed early drafts of chapters that centered on their teachings, and Joseph steered me clear of a few confusing ideas of my own. Emmanuel Ghent made Winnicott's writings accessible to me over the years, and he was enormously helpful at the moment that "going on being" dawned in my mind. Phyllis Ehrenthal kindly reviewed an early draft and provided invaluable comments, while Amy Gross gave time and energy to the manuscript and helped it tremendously. Jody Shields and John House generously traded inspirational readings and conversation with me. Daniel Goleman brought Abhidharma alive for me years ago and has continued to make it relevant in subsequent discussions. Rob Stein and Helen Tworkov were always encouraging, and George Lange, Kiki, and Barry have been there for the whole project. Anne Edelstein provided invaluable assistance and friendship, while Marion Stroud's interest and support was much appreciated. My wife, Arlene, is the most constant, and hidden, influence in this work. She inspired, accompanied, and encouraged me both during the writing of it and throughout our precious time together. To her, Sonia, Will, Frank, Sherrie, Jean, Dave, and Sheila. Finally, I wish to thank the people I have worked with over the years. Their willingness to engage in the clouds of unknowing has been a great blessing in my life.

1. Lawrence Shainberg, *Ambivalent Zen: A Memoir* (New York: Pantheon Books, 1996), pp. 141–144.

2. See volume 2 of Frederick Perls, Ralph Hefferline, and Paul Goodman's *Gestalt Therapy* (New York: Bantam Books, 1951), p. 483. Volume 2 of this text was written by Paul Goodman and contains the clearest exposition of the theory of Gestalt therapy that I have found.

3. D. W. Winnicott, "Ego Integration in Child Development" (1962) in *The Maturational Processes and the Facilitating Environment* (New York: International Universities Press, 1965), p. 60.

4. Jack Kornfield, *After the Ecstasy, the Laundry* (New York: Bantam Books, 2000).

5. *The Way of Lao Tzu (Tao-te Ching)*, trans. Wing-Tsit Chan (Indianapolis & New York: Bobbs-Merrill, 1963), p. 225.

6. From a chapter entitled "Mind" in the *Dhammapada*, trans. P. Lal (New York: Farrar, Strauss & Giroux, 1967), pp. 49–50.

7. W. R. Bion, *Attention and Interpretation* (London: Tavistock, 1970), p. 42.

8. Michael Eigen, *The Psychoanalytic Mystic* (London: Free Association Books, 1998), pp. 39–40.

9. For the source of this quote, and for a wonderful portrait of Bion's contributions, see Eigen's *Psychoanalytic Mystic* (London: Free Association Books, 1998), p. 81. The quote itself is from W. R. Bion, *Transformations* (New York: Jason Aronson, 1965/1983), p. 148.

10. See Ram Dass, *The Only Dance There Is* (Garden City: Anchor Books, 1974), pp. 108–113.

11. Ram Dass, *Grist For the Mill* (with Stephen Levine) (Santa Cruz: Unity Press, 1976), pp. 73–74.

12. See Stephen Batchelor, *The Awakening of the West: The Encounter of Buddhism and Western Culture* (Berkeley: Parallax Press, 1994), pp. 3–15.

13. E. J. Thomas (ed.), *Buddhist Scriptures* (London: John Murray, 1913), pp. 118–122.

14. Michael Eigen, *Psychic Deadness* (New York: Jason Aronson, 1996).

15. Bhadantacariya Buddhaghosa, *The Path of Purification (Visuddhimagga)*, trans. Bhikkhu Nanamoli (Berkeley & London: Shambhala, 1976), p. 152.

16. *The Life of the Buddha According to the Pali Canon*, trans. & ed. Bhikkhu Nanamoli (Kandy, Sri Lanka: Buddhist Publication Society, 1972), p. 18.

17. Ibid., p. 21. Also see Roberto Calasso's *Ka: Stories of the Mind and Gods of India* (New York: Vintage Books, 1998) for a discussion of this episode in the Buddha's life.

18. For more on the Buddha's drive for a greater individualism, see Robert Thurman's *Inner Revolution* (New York: Riverhead, 1998).

19. Kalu Rinpoche, *The Dharma* (Albany: State University of New York Press, 1986), p. 113.

20. For this discussion of the *kleshas* I am indebted to a correspondence with Stephen Batchelor. For more on Shantideva, see his translation of *A Guide to the Boddhisattva's Way of Life (Bodhicaryavatāra)* (Dharamsala, India: Library of Tibetan Works and Archives, 1979).

21. D. W. Winnicott, "Birth Memories, Birth Trauma, and Anxiety" (1949) in *Through Paediatrics to Psycho-Analysis: Collected Papers* (New York: Bruner/Mazel, 1958, 1992), pp. 182–183.

22. For an account of this incident, see Russell Shorto's *Saints and Madmen: Breaking Down the Barriers Between Psychiatry and Spirituality* (New York: Henry Holt, 1999), pp. 78–80.

23. Walpola Rahula, *What the Buddha Taught* (New York: Grove Press, 1959/1974), p. 65.

24. *Shobogenzo: Zen Essays by Dogen*, trans. Thomas Cleary (Honolulu: University of Hawaii Press, 1986), p. 19.

25. For more on this, see Michael Eigen, *The Psychoanalytic Mystic*, pp. 92–94, and *Psychic Deadness*, pp. 69–88.

26. Michael Eigen, "Feeling Normal" in *Toxic Nourishment* (London: Karnac Books, 1999), p. 87.

27. Jack Kornfield, *Living Buddhist Masters* (Santa Cruz: Unity Press, 1977), p. 19.

28. *The Dhammapada*, trans. P. Lal (New York: Farrar, Straus & Giroux, 1967), p. 115.

29. Ibid., p. 127.

30. Jack Kornfield, *A Path with Heart: A Guide Through the Perils and Promises of Spiritual Life* (New York: Bantam, 1993), pp. 108–110.

31. See Michael Eigen's "Originary *Jouissance*," in his *Psychoanalytic Mystic*, p. 136.

32. *Anguttara Nikaya: Discourses of the Buddha, An Anthology*, trans. Nyanaponika Thera (Kandy, Sri Lanka: Buddhist Publication Society, 1975).

33. Buddhaghosa, *The Path of Purification (Visuddhimagga)*, pp. 149–150.

34. Stephen A. Mitchell, "Psychoanalysis and the Degradation of Romance," *Psychoanalytic Dialogues* 7, no. 1 (1977): 24. See also his *Can Love Last? The Fate of Romance Over Time* (New York & London: W. W. Norton, 2002).

35. Buddhaghosa, *The Path of Purification (Visuddhimagga)*, p. 752.

36. Ibid., p. 753.

37. Soma Thera, *The Way of Mindfulness* (Kandy, Sri Lanka: Buddhist Publication Society, 1941/1981), p. 24.

38. For these descriptions and more, see Marilyn M. Rhie and Robert A. F. Thurman, *Worlds of Transformation: Tibetan Art of Wisdom and Compassion* (New York: Tibet House New York in association with the Shelley and Donald Rubin Foundation & Harry N. Abrams, Distributors, 1999), pp. 37–44. Quotes from p. 39.

39. *The Life of the Buddha According to the Pali Canon*, p. 324.

40. Allen Wheelis, *How People Change* (New York: Harper Colophon, 1973), p. 113.

ABOUT THE AUTHOR

MARK EPSTEIN, M.D., is a psychiatrist in private practice and the author of *Going to Pieces without Falling Apart, Thoughts without a Thinker, Open to Desire,* and *Psychotherapy without the Self.* He lives in New York City.

Photo by Larry Bercow

ABOUT WISDOM PUBLICATIONS

Wisdom Publications, a nonprofit publisher, is dedicated to making available authentic works relating to Buddhism for the benefit of all. We publish books by ancient and modern masters in all traditions of Buddhism, translations of important texts, and original scholarship. Additionally, we offer books that explore East-West themes unfolding as traditional Buddhism encounters our modern culture in all its aspects. Our titles are published with the appreciation of Buddhism as a living philosophy, and with the special commitment to preserve and transmit important works from Buddhism's many traditions.

To learn more about Wisdom, or to browse books online, visit our website at www.wisdompubs.org.

You may request a copy of our catalog online or by writing to this address:

Wisdom Publications
199 Elm Street
Somerville, Massachusetts 02144 USA
Telephone: 617-776-7416
Fax: 617-776-7841
Email: info@wisdompubs.org
www.wisdompubs.org

THE WISDOM TRUST

As a nonprofit publisher, Wisdom is dedicated to the publication of Dharma books for the benefit of all sentient beings and dependent upon the kindness and generosity of sponsors in order to do so. If you would like to make a donation to Wisdom, you may do so through our website or our Somerville office. If you would like to help sponsor the publication of a book, please write or email us at the address above.

Thank you.

Wisdom is a nonprofit, charitable 501(c)(3) organization affiliated with the Foundation for the Preservation of the Mahayana Tradition (FPMT).